G000150722

Coastal Trade
of the Ketch Millbay
# of Plymouth between
1902-44

Lulu Chesnutt

Coastal Trade of the Ketch Millbay of Plymouth between 1902-44.

by Lulu Chesnutt©

ISBN-10: 0-9553681-0-3
ISBN-13: 978-0-9553681-0-3

Published by Lulu Chesnutt
15 River Rd., Lambeg, Lisburn, N.I.

Printed by Browne Printers Ltd.
Port Rd. Letterkenny, Co. Donegal, R.O.I.
Tel.: 0048353749121387
e-mail: reception@browneprinters.com

In Memory of Johnny Chesnutt,
Johnny Goût
and the Mariners
of Derrylaghan
and Teelin.

1914 Millbay of Plymouth Reg 48

Date	Voyage	tons	Cargo	Arr
Jan 27	Campbeltown to Irvine		Ballast	Arr 27th
Feb 10	Irvine to Campbeltown	103	Corsehill House Coal	Arr 10th
23	Campbeltown to Irvine		Ballast	Arr 23
Mar 7	Irvine to Campbeltown	101	Corsehill House Coal	1rs 8th
22	Campbeltown to Irvine		Ballast	Arr 22
24	Irvine to Carnlough	105	Montgomery field coal	Arr 27
April 8	Carnlough to Dublin	105	Whiting	Arr 15
May 6	Dublin to Castletown		(Part Carg) Manure	Arr 7
17	Inspected at Castletown 9.6.1914		11 tuns off with remainder	Arr 19
12	Castletown to Ramsey	04	Sa...	June
19	Ramsey to Belmullet		Ball...	18
June 18	Belmullet to Mullaghmore		Kelp	Arr 30
25	Mullaghmore to Bowling		Ballast	Arr 9 July
July 9	Bowling to Greenock			
12	Greenock to Feelin	01	House Coals	Arr 15
August 4	Feelin to Buncrana		Ballast	Arr 17th
25	Buncrana to Campbeltown	68	Peat	Arr 26
Sep 2	Campbeltown to Irvine		Ballast	Arr 3 Sep
8	Irvine to Donegal	101	Montgomery field coal	October

H.M. CUSTOMS 2 JUL 1914 BOWLING

TABLE OF CONTENTS

Biography of Ship

At the beginning of the twentieth century a large proportion of the world's trade was still carried by sail and in the years before road transport became cost effective, most Irish ports had fleets of small coastal trading ships, many of whose rigs could be comparable to this description by Joseph Conrad:

> The fore-and-aft rig in its simplicity and the beauty of
> its aspect under every angle of vision, is, I believe,
> unapproachable.
> A schooner, a yawl, or cutter in charge of a capable man
> seems to handle herself as if endowed with the power of
> reasoning and the gift of sweet execution (Conrad 38).

This is a portrayal of one such vessel, the *Millbay of Plymouth*, a small wooden merchant ketch later fitted with an auxiliary engine, trading between Ireland and Great Britain during a period spanning two World Wars. This study is based on the vessel's original log book and reflects an example of Irish coastal and cross-channel trade in an age that necessitated ships of this size working as cheaply as possible between small harbours with few facilities and taking on board whatever cargo became available. This therefore is a snapshot of maritime activity revealing the specialised seafaring way of life of a by-gone age that has now been surpassed by modern marine technology and transportation.

The *Millbay of Plymouth* was built in 1880 in East Stonehouse, Plymouth, Devon. The vessel derived her name from the Millbay area adjacent to Plymouth Docks and evidence of her construction in a shipyard in this locality can be gleaned from the minutes of the Great Western Dock Company's ledgers in 1862. This document indicates that Charles Francis Williams was given "a piece of ground in the north west corner of the outer basin extending in length 120 feet by 35 feet breadth".[1]

An existing map shows a shipyard in this vicinity (Appendix A).

The *Millbay's* surviving cargo-log dates from 1902 and ends with her sale as a trading vessel in 1944 (Appendix B). The following extract taken from the West Devon Record Office of Plymouth Ship Registers details her registration, tonnage capacity together with a record of ownership within the period specified:

> Ketch Millbay Official Number 83941
> No.32 1880 November 18th Built by Charles Francis
> Williams, East
> Stonehouse 1880.
> Registered tonnage 64.74 Length 72'5 Breadth 19'2
> Depth in hold 8'4

---

1 The National Archives (NA) PRO COPY, Rail 857/5 Plymouth Great Western Dock Minute Book 2,
   June 1860 – January 1874

Owners John Nicholas Roose 32 shares Thomas Robert
Roose 32 shares
Shipowners of Plymouth.

May 19th 1887 sold to Charles and Nat Winder of
Plymouth, Master
Mariners, 32 shares each.

February 9th 1899 sold to John Cully of Portavogie,
County Down, Merchant
64 shares.

January 14th 1901 sold to John Rooney of Kilkeel, County
Down,
Merchant, 64 shares.

April 7th 1902 registered anew upon alteration of hull.
Certificate delivered up and cancelled.

Nov.7 1902 John Rooney 64 shares.

May 16 1906 sold to Thomas Doyle of Kilkeel, County
Down, Master
Mariner, 64 shares.

November 23rd 1912 sold to Hugh Chesnutt of
Derrylaghan, Cilcar (sic),
Master Mariner, 64 shares.

Certificate closed registry cancelled May 15th 1927 in
consequence of a change in means of propulsion.
Nov. 7 1927 Hugh Chesnutt 64 shares. Registered
tonnage 42.38 ketch,
Straight stern, wood pleasure yacht. Length 72'6
Breadth 19'2 Depth in hold 8'2. Internal combustion
engine L.Gardiner & Sons Ltd. Diesel 40 hp.

January 8th 1933 Hugh Chesnutt dies intestate.
June 13th 1944 William Thomas Chesnutt sold 64 shares
to John James Chesnutt.

August 8th 1944 John James Chesnutt sold 64 shares to
Douglas Albert Hooper of Ross on Wye, Road Haulage
Contractor. [2]

Under the *Millbay's* terms of ownership the shareholding system outlined above
was a requirement laid down by the Merchant Shipping Acts whereby ships such
as this were owned by shareholders holding between them the 64 shares into
which vessel property was divided by the Merchant Shipping Acts (Greenhill *The*

[2] West Devon Record Office, 2907/1/3/5 Plymouth Ship Registers

Merchant Schooners 29). As Greenhill suggests, there might be for example, any number of shareholders from one to 64, but usually a dozen or more and sometimes single shares were held jointly (29). There was always a legal managing owner who often was the inspiration of the enterprise and who might be a shipbuilder, local mill or timber yard owner, country banker, shipmaster or a broker. Usually the shareholders came from the local community of the sea or riverside village or the small town from which the ship sailed and they could include the master, as was the case in the *Millbay's* ownership. One example of this early twentieth century shareholding system is highlighted by Greenhill when he points out that the wife and brother of the Prime Minister of the day David Lloyd George, were shareholders in Porthmadog schooners in the early years of the century (30).

In 1890 British merchant sailing vessels registered as of ports in the United Kingdom totalled just under three million tons net. In the same year some 171,000 tons of shipping was listed in Lloyds Register as schooner or ketch-rigged and registered at a home port in the United Kingdom. As Greenhill states a conservative estimate would add approximately 50% to the Lloyd's total to include vessels registered under the Merchant Shipping Acts but not listed by Lloyds. The total tonnage of schooners from United Kingdom ports was therefore very roughly some 7½% of all sailing vessel tonnage registered at United Kingdom home ports in 1890 (31).

Confirmation of the respective ownership of the *Millbay* by the Doyle and Chesnutt families is reflected in the following extracts: one entry that appears in Lloyds Shipping Register in 1911, another is taken from the Mercantile Navy List of 1936 which also signifies tonnage and code changes:

ALPHABETICAL LIST OF BRITISH REGISTERED SAILING VESSELS

Official No.	Name of Ship And Port of Registry	Rig	Where Built	When Built	International Code, Signal	Reg. Tonnage	Owner, or Part Owner, and Manager X Signifies *Managing Owner* Italics signify *Manager*
83941	*Millbay*, Plymouth	K	Stonehouse	1880	T.W.B.N	49	James Doyle, Kilkeel, Co. Down.

ALPHABETICAL LIST OF BRITISH REGISTERD SAILING VESSELS

Official No.	Name of Ship And Port of Registry	Rig	Where and When Built	International Code, Signal	Reg. Tonnage	Owner, or Part Owner, and Manager X Signifies *Managing Owner* Italics signify *Manager*
83941	*Millbay*, Plymouth	K	Stonehouse 1880	M.F.Y.F	45	William T. Chesnutt, Derrylaghan, Kilcar, Co. Donegal John J. Chesnutt, same address

3

Although early trading references in the log-book relating to the years 1902 and 1903 are somewhat faded and partially illegible, it is nevertheless possible to

---

3 E-mail from Charles McCarthy, Point Road, Dundalk (23ʳᵈ October 2004)

discern that around this period and onwards the *Millbay* under the captaincy of John Rooney was consistently carrying out trading operations involving the transportation of granite and coal between Annalong and Kilkeel and the west coast of England, as reflected in an extract from the log in 1904:

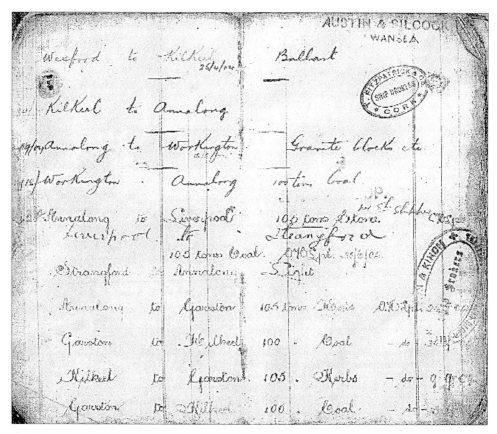

Fig. 1.
The Cargo Book showing passages in 1904

In 1906 the *Millbay* was sold by John Rooney to the Doyle family of Kilkeel and in a recent meeting with Captain Gerry Doyle, great nephew of James Doyle her former owner, he identified his ancestor's handwriting in the log-book, thus confirming his family's long association with the Kilkeel and Annalong coastal trade. He also stated that they were typical of many families in this area for whom the merchant coastal trade was the traditional way of life at the beginning of the twentieth century (Doyle).

The villages of Annalong and Kilkeel were therefore well-known ports for the export of Mourne granite in the early years of the century. From here the *Millbay* left with cargoes of kerbstones and granite setts measuring around five or six cubic inches mainly for use in the paving of English city streets such as Liverpool in the days before reinforced concrete was introduced (Doyle). Confirmation of the exportation of granite and importation of coal into the Mourne area is also verified by Elizabeth McBride, whose father Bob Cousins, was a coal merchant in Annalong during this period. This lady also provided the following information concerning the *Millbay's* involvement in this trade as revealed in the following extract taken from Annalong and Kilkeel Harbour Book Records:

> 19.7.02 Kilkeel to Liverpool 75 tons of Granite
> Harbour dues of 12/-
> Cargo dues on Reg. Tonnage 6/3
>
> 18.5.03 Workington to Kilkeel – 80 tons of Coal.
>
> 7. 6.03 100 tons Granite – Dues on Granite 8/4 tonnage 6/8

(McBride)

In addition to the export of granite, the growing of potatoes was prolific in the Annalong area and while very low at the beginning of the century, these exports increased after 1905 (Fitzpatrick 27). Although most of the vessels appear to have arrived in Annalong light, Harbour Records confirm an average of about twenty including the *Millbay* bringing coal for use into the area (McBride). However it is evident that although based at Annalong and Kilkeel and primarily trading in coal and granite, this vessel was also involved in carrying various other commodities which caused her to be absent from her home port over long periods. For example between January and August 1910 she is recorded carrying cargoes as diverse as salt, manure and timber between areas as far apart as Waterford in southern Ireland, Ramsey in the Isle of Man and Port William in western Scotland, where she is pictured at anchor:

Fig. 2.
The Harbour, Port William with "Millbay" lying at the quayside

The textile towns of Lancashire and Yorkshire had as Greenhill and Gifford point out been connected by canal with Liverpool since1820 as well as being linked to the developing industrial midlands and potteries of Staffordshire (Greenhill and Gifford *Victorian and Edwardian Ships* 92). Harbours were therefore developing and dock facilities improving as smaller ports of the north prospered in the nineteenth century. Among these were Maryport, Whitehaven and Workington where as the *Millbay's* cargo log records, large quantities of coal were also being exported to other ports on Ireland's eastern coast such as Clogherhead, Dublin, Skerries and Wexford (Appendix B). In the same way Connah's Quay in North Wales owed its development to the export of bricks and as Greenhill asserts, this town was the last port in Wales to own sailing ships (Greenhill *The Merchant Schooners* 183). Glazed earthen-ware pipes from Lancashire and ceramic sanitary products from the Staffordshire potteries were also exported to Ireland from this port, therefore sailing ships such as the *Millbay* were a most suitable means for the transportation of these commodities because owing to their fragility it was essential that they be loaded slowly and carefully by hand (Appendix B).

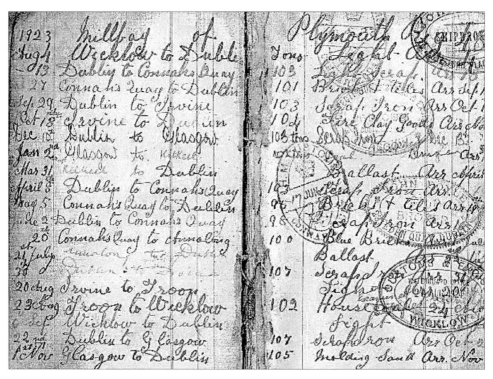

Fig. 3.
Pages from the Certified Cargo Book of 1923

As Latham also states, the brick trade was one of the last refuges of sailing ships because steamers required quick turnaround times in port and fast passages in all weathers in order to earn their keep (Latham 102). In a further analysis on the persistence of sail in the face of the growing competition from steam-powered vessels, Greenhill highlights the diminishing, albeit tenacity of sail, asserting that in 1900 British sail tonnage was still over two million tons. However by 1910 this was reduced to just over one million compared with ten and a half million tons of steam-powered ships (Greenhill. *The Ship* 48). Nevertheless for short sea voyages vessels using sails continued to trade and by 1914 there were a number of small vessels that had been equipped with auxiliary engines which he argues "prolonged the life of the small sailing ship until the middle of the century and beyond" (qtd. in Greenhill 55). Slade also concurs with this view by also pointing out that the life of coasting ketches were prolonged for a generation after World War I mainly due to the installation of auxiliary diesel engines (Slade 31). Therefore, while the investment in a vessel of the *Millbay's* tonnage was low, often carrying cargoes into remote areas where bad land communications existed as was the case in many of the secluded areas in western Ireland where she operated later on, a ketch such as this propelled by an auxiliary engine with a hardworking master who was a shareholder with little shore overheads could operate profitably. On the other hand the economics of coasting with power in years of depression would have been difficult as was the case later in the century when during intervals in 1932,1933 and 1934 the ship was laid up:

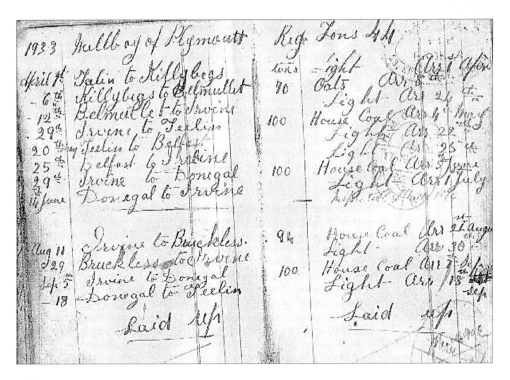

Fig. 4.
Certified Cargo Book 1933

However, whenever possible during these slump years many masters like that of the *Millbay* frequently used the wind thereby saving fuel (McShane). These factors points to one of the reasons why this vessel, apart from the short periods of recession alluded to above, appears to have operated economically until requisitioned by the British Government for merchant service later on during World War II.

In the remote south western region of Donegal in the shadow of Sliabh-a-Liag, Europe's highest sea cliff, lies the small harbour of Teelin situated on the western bank of the Glen River estuary:

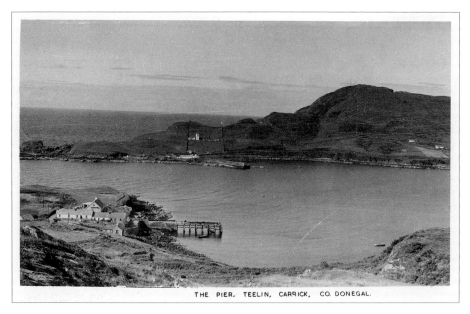

THE PIER, TEELIN, CARRICK, CO. DONEGAL.

Fig. 5.
The Pier, Teelin in background

On the eastern side of the bay is another small harbour, Claddaghnageera, where the *Millbay* also berthed and discharged cargo:

In this vicinity the surrounding jagged windswept coastline of quartzite rock presented sailors with an acute reminder that these rocky headlands held

Fig. 6.
The Pier, Claddaghnageera

formidable navigational hazards for sailing ships entering a seascape that could well be reminiscent of the expected Landfall alluded to in Conrad's *The Mirror of the Sea*:

> In all the devious tracings the course of a sailing
> ship leaves upon the white paper of a chart she is
> always aiming for that one little spot – maybe a small
> island in the ocean, a single headland upon the long
> coast of a continent… maybe a Lighthouse on a bluff…
> or simply the peaked form of a Mountain like an ant
> heap afloat upon the waters (Conrad 3).

In the following extract Phelan also emphasises the unexpected dangers sailing ships were exposed to while navigating Donegal's tortuous coastline:

> Slieve League and the off-lying island of Rathlin O'Birne
> grew on the bow… the narrows between the cliffs and
> the island produced false winds which flogged the jib,
> snatched at the forestay and shook the mast. The waves
> came rolling up astern, growing steeper and steeper
> until an individual roller could no longer support its
> own mass and a small crest toppled forward and came
> sliding down the wavefront, a self generating roll of
> foam (Phelan 155).

Towards the end of the nineteenth century one area of improvement that the government was responsible for was the construction by the Congested Districts Board of harbours in certain deprived areas along Ireland's western seaboard that included Co. Donegal (Bardon 169). One example of this is depicted on a stone slab still visible at the entrance to Killybegs pier, which bears the following inscription:

> Erected by the Board of Works
> From Funds
> Provided by Parliament
> And
> The Congested Districts Board
> 1896-1897

Despite possessing the best harbour on the west coast at that time Killybegs had according to Conaghan, no added advantage or facilities for ships. As he asserts "its two stone piers were tidal and sailing boats often found it impossible to get out of the harbour in the prevailing south-west winds" (qtd. in Conaghan 21). Although it could be argued that Teelin and Killybegs were nevertheless good deep harbour estuaries allowing easy discharge of cargoes for vessels of the *Millbay's* tonnage, maritime access to other small harbours in the locality would have presented certain difficulties for sailing ships. Further inland on the northern side of Donegal Bay there is a fairly shallow approach governed by high water that tends to dry out at low tide. At Mullinasole, near Donegal Town pictured below, for example, there is a very shallow estuary that is determined by tides and this meant access for ships to small harbours such as this were tied to a high water approach.

Fig. 7.
The Pier, Killybegs

Fig. 8.
The Pier, Mullinasole

Because no professional pilots existed in this area at that time to guide ships into these tricky locations the question of draught and the vessel's ability to access any of these minor estuaries at various states of the tide would have been known only to those who had an intricate knowledge of the local navigational problems. Therefore the window of opportunity for the safe delivery of cargoes was severely limited without this local insight and unless vessels of this size had the ability to dry out on these estuaries and refloat at high water, opportunities for coastal trade would have been severely restricted. (Appendix C).

Therefore not only did tidal influence play an important part in the navigational operations of a sailing ship, the wind too was a crucial and relevant factor. Joseph Conrad writes of the significance of the prevailing westerly wind for those under sail:

> The west wind reigns over the seas surrounding the
> coast of these kingdoms; and from the gateway of the
> channels, from promontories as if from watch-towers,
> from estuaries of rivers as if from postern gates, from
> passage-ways, inlets, straits, firths, the garrison of the
> Isle and the crews of the ships going and returning look
> to the westward to judge by the varied splendours of his
> sunset mantle the mood of that arbitrary ruler
> (Conrad 126).

At the beginning of the twentieth century Teelin was also the home port to a fleet of smacks plying between Sligo and coastal ports of Mayo when before the adoption of the schooner and ketch rigs, these single-mast smacks were the most common small merchant sailing vessel. One such craft, the *Mere de Misericorde* acquired by Hugh Chesnutt in 1890, also carried out cross-channel trade. This vessel was later sunk by a steamer while riding at anchor at King's Cross Ferry, Arran in Scotland, and in 1912 he replaced this smack with the ketch *Millbay* which he also based at Teelin (Chesnutt). Hugh Chesnutt's initial crew included his son, Johnny who later became master, John Griffin and Condy Donegan, all local seamen, three of whom are pictured here:

Fig.9.
Condy Donegan,
Johnny Chesnutt,
Hugh Chesnutt

Later in 1920 Ned Williams, a native of the Island of St. Helena in the South Atlantic, joined the crew as a cook. (McShane). He is pictured along with three other crew members:

Fig. 10.
Johnny Chesnutt, John James Watson, Ned Williams, Ned Cunningham
Courtesy Catherine Cunningham, Kille, Kilcar.

Fig, 11
James Mc Shane, Archie Linton

The arrival of a coloured man to this remote region of Donegal was for many people their first encounter with a person of another race. An example of local reaction to this cultural experience is recalled by Moira Cunningham of Claddaghnageera, Kilcar and Brigid Cannon of Portachran, Kilcar who stated that as young children they were apprehensive when they encountered Ned Williams in their neighbourhood and they tended to avoid meeting him. However Catherine Cunningham whose father Edward (Ned) pictured above was a member of the *Millbay*'s crew by this time and consequently better acquainted with the sailor from St. Helena, recalled that Ned Williams often brought along a gramophone to their home for the benefit of the children's entertainment. As she put it "we had great fun when Ned pointed out to us children that there was a wee man inside the box speaking to us" (qtd. Catherine Cunningham). It would therefore appear that Williams overcame any prejudice if indeed any existed, and soon became integrated into the local community of Teelin and Derrylaghan. This affinity is also highlighted by Mary McGeown of Kilcar who recalled that during a prolonged period ashore when his ship was laid up, Ned who lived in the Chesnutt family home during his interval ashore, taught her mother and other women in the neighbourhood many cooking skills. She recalled for example, that it was he who taught them how to bake Christmas fruit cakes including a particular favourite as she related "I remember a big round plum pudding steamed in a flour-bag that my mother then shared out with whoever called at our house" (qtd. McGeown). It therefore appears that this man was a valued member of the *Millbay's* crew and this was further evidenced when he later fell ill he was brought to hospital in Belfast aboard the *Millbay* by Johnny Chesnutt in order that he might receive the best possible medical attention and when he subsequently died his remains were interred in Belfast's City Cemetery (McShane).

Among other local crew-members employed later on were James McShane, his sons Pack (Patrick) and Michael Thomas, all natives of Doire Leathan (Derrylaghan) Kilcar. In the following interview given to the author at his home in Cloghan, Brockagh, near Ballybofey, Co. Donegal the *Millbay's* last surviving crew member, Michael Thomas McShane recalled life on board the vessel:

Fig. 11.
Michael Thomas McShane in 1942 and today

Q. Michael, I know your father James and brother Pack, were already crew members on the *Millbay,* but tell me when did you first join them on a voyage?

A. That was in 1942 taking a cargo of coal from Irvine to Carrickfergus and Teelin, but I left her temporarily in Carrickfergus because I was wanted at home.

Q. How long was your father on the *Millbay?*

A. Oh, from I was a wee gasur.

Q. Who else had worked on her? What crew was on the *Millbay?*

A. Only myself and Pack and my father when I was on her. When I left her I got a man out in Carrickfergus who had been a fisherman – well the War was on at the time , he was building air-raid shelters. I was up the town and I saw this man, I knew him. I was leaving the *Millbay* at the time. I told him Johnny had no one but my father so I came down and told Johnny about this man and he said "Oh take him down" – a man from St. John's Point, Danny McCallig – he was drowned after that. There was another man on her by the name of Paddy Doyle, a wee Scotch fella was on her by the name of George Wilson and there was another fine big man on her, Archie Linton.

Q. What about Ned Williams, where did they get him?

A. He came to them from Scotland as a cook, he came from St. Helena.

Q. Did Ned do all the cooking on board?

A. Oh aye, and he did plenty of work too.

Q. Didn't Ned die eventually?

A. Oh he did – he was dying in fact when I went into him in Doire Leathan. He was taken down on the horse and cart to the Point of the Claggan – he took sick up at the house in Doire Leathan - of diabetes I think he died. They took him to hospital in Belfast on the *Millbay*.

Q. Did you all have different jobs?

A. Well Johnny was looking to us, I was on the guy ropes when the buckets went down… I was on the ropes in case they went out too fast… then there was a man up on the ladder. Pack was on the ropes then and when Pack left I went on the ropes winching it up.

Q. What did Johnny do?

A. Oh, mostly at the engine, he was mostly at the wheel too as well……my father too, they took it in turns. Johnny was very funny at night you know, oh, cripes it was all telling yarns about home, all old reels.

Q. Michael, was the *Millbay* an all-wooden boat?

A. Of course she was, the whole lot, sure I used to have to go out and scrape the bow of her when she would be on dry ground – to scrape the shells off her if she would be moored for a long time.

Q. She appears to have been laid up for a long time, why was that?

A. Oh well, no work, no cargoes, waiting to get a cargo.

Q. Did she always have an engine?

A. Oh no, O Dhia no, as a schooner she was built. There were two berths in her, two cabins in her. The deckhands had one cabin and Johnny the other. Then we got an engine, then the engine was put down and all hands were put into the one cabin.

Q. When did they get the engine installed?

A. Oh, I'm not fit to answer that.

Q. Was it a big engine?

A. No, about 40 hp. I think it was.

Q. What was it run on?

A. Oh diesel I suppose, she never had an engine before this, she was a ketch, the ketch *Millbay*.

Q. Were you ever sea-sick on board, was it ever rough?

A. Oh you would be standing at the wheel and the sea over you and it would go out again. I was never sea-sick in my life in it. I remember Johnny and my father, the two of them getting sea-sick, I was left at the wheel of the boat.

Q. How did you know where you were going Michael, in order to steer.

A. The compass was there facing me, so I could see the set course.

Q. What did you have to do, say coming back from Scotland?

A. Well, when the cargo of coal was in, in Scotland, before they hove to, the minute the whole lot was in she was battened down. Then we had to scrub the whole boat clean when the cargo was discharged. We had to lift buckets of water off the side. On a Saturday evening down below it would be scrubbed white with Vim and with a scrubbing brush……you couldn't do that with a bucket half full of water!

Q. How long did it take you to get from Scotland to Carrickfergus?

A. Oh not long, with tail wind..I shovelled coal in her in Scotland. I helped to put in a   cargo of coal in a wee place called Tarbert in Scotland, we couldn't get no men, an army man was the only one we could get and Johnny asked me would I help. I would do anything for the money I would. Oh if my father ever was on her I helped to put out cargoes of coal here in Teelin, myself and Peter Cunnea, and up at Bruckless unloading her, we used to go up to Bruckless.

Q. What way did he pay you, did he pay you by the hour?

A. For the cargo of coal?

Q. Yes.

A. He paid whatever was for putting out the cargo of coal you got it, you see there was so much to be got. Johnny had nothing to do with that, it wasn't him paid that, no it was the man who was getting the coal. Carmichael's was the name, they paid when the cargo was out… so I was away out with the 'sheriff' to the house (much laughter) I remember it well, for my money! Johnny's way (of payment) was out of the different cargoes on shares, divided between his father and my father.

Q. What was the food like on the way back from Scotland?

A. The food, oh cripes the food was good. Oh it was good, it was mostly salty fish, we would boil them. Dhia, the fish they call the skate – the two wings on them – Johnny used to cut the two wings off and dry them up and myself and him ate them! Pack wouldn't eat them, oh no.

Q. Was she ever overhauled, Michael, did she have to be maintained?

A. No, the engine gave up once only, but he got it going in a short time, must have got an engine-man or engineer out.

Q. Was it a hard life?

A. On the boat – oh indeed it was, there was not much rest.

Q. Who worked the sails?

A. Oh well, every man for himself, it was everyone's job, did we get wet… big heavy canvas… and do you know, out on the jib you had to stand on a rope… they came the whole way out the last time out to Claddaghnageera from Scotland, and when my father went up to let out the jib the rope broke and he went out into the tide, he could swim and swam round and got a hold of the chain. I remember him telling of Johnny calling 'where are you, James, where are you?' – he (Johnny) brought down the ladder and got him up and the only thing that bothered my father – Johnny used to tell it – was that his tobacco got all wet in his pocket!

(At this point, Irene Coyle, Michael's daughter, joined the interview)

IC. What about the loaves of bread?… tell her all…

A. Cripes, this was in Irvine. We were ready to go out and the grocers came down all the time with supplies before going out. A wee young fella came down with a hand-cart with six white loaves in two baskets. I got cheeky enough at the time you see, what I should have done was thrown out a wee light mooring to him and he could tie it to the baskets, but I was too conceited in myself and I threw him a hook. Each time the basket pushed past I tried to grab it and down it took. I made a grab for the basket but as I moved too fast over the top of my head went the basket and I fell in between the boat and the pier and when I came up – I had a pair of old waders on up to that – and as I came up the basket was going down, but I was a good swimmer at the time, I got the basket. I took out the six loaves, the six loaves was dried at the fire at the wee stove and wee slices were cut. Many and many a time Pack said "a charity if you were drowned"!

IC. What about the rats that used to be in it?

A. Oh, the rats coming in on the ropes? – oh aye, black rats. How we used to scatter them was to split a round tin lid and put it in on the ropes, they couldn't get past that, they used to be after the potato skins. There was a wee monkey too on another boat tied beside us, he used to come in as well,… steal the cabbage out of the tin, and he away like hell out again, oh there were some good times then too. Food, we used to eat the spuds that was left over in the evening. Oh the spuds from the dinner… when I was there first any spuds that was left over I would throw them away. Cripes I had a lock of spuds I covered up to throw them to the rats – the rats were mad for them – so tae-time came and Johnny said "where's them spuds Michael?"… I told him… "Oh Jove, you should have kept them and fried them for the tae"… he nearly ate *me!*

Q. Was it dangerous on board?

A. Oh it was if you didn't know what you were at, it was.

Q. Was that your first time at sea, that time you came across from Scotland?

A. It was, but of course I used to fish on local boats, in fact I was the main man in the boat that we fished out of Teelin. I had two brothers, Pack and Dan, who were with me, 'twas lines we were fishing, baskets of lines, several hundred hooks, not one of them would venture to put out the hooks, 'twas myself, sure we fished out to St. John's Point along with ones from Killybegs in open boats.

Q. What was it like sleeping on board the *Millbay*?

A. The bed was the most rickety – I was down below my father with me – you just had to lie on your side.

Q. Were these the bunks?

A. Yes.

Q. What were they like?

A. Oh, just a bag of sawdust that was the mattress, that was it, oh it was rough.

Q. What kind of lighting had they on board at night.

A. No light at all, just two lamps for showing on every side, that's why they lost the court case when the steam boat hit them. Johnny was just up with the lamp to hang it out when he was hit – that was on the other boat – 6 minutes too late, so they lost the case – they had just time to get out, very lucky. They went out next day in the punt, I heard him telling it, with a boat-hook. There was a big hole in her side and he got in the boat-hook and he pulled out an old blanket and that blanket was in the *Millbay* yet… now…

Q. How did they remove the coal from Teelin Pier?

A. Oh on carts, Lily the mare carted the coal. Dan Byrne too was carting out to Kilcar. Over in Teelin the Jones' had horses and carts too.

Q. Did the boat have to be inspected at all?

A. I don't think so, no, but when the War was on, that time the army were around.

Q. Was there any smuggling going on?

A. Oh, no definitely not.

Q. Michael, thank you very much for taking the time to talk to me.

As can be seen from this crewman's account, conditions on board the *Millbay* were crude and cramped; there was no limit to the working hours, they lacked social security, they had no entitlement to designated holidays, recruitment was on an ad hoc basis and health and safety conditions were practically non existent. It also appears they had to be able to do all but major maintenance on board because the owners were reluctant to pay others what they themselves could do. On the other hand as this vessel's crew were for the most part made up of local Donegal men with home ties, both master and crew were drawn from the same working class background. In this account it is also apparent that some crew members had an investment in the vessel and stood to benefit directly from her profitable operations. On the whole although industrial conditions were still very primitive, they appear to have been better in smaller vessels such as this in such matters of food, the nature of the work and the good relationship between master and seamen. Another advantage was the fact that there were certain opportunities for young crew members with the initiative displayed by Michael McShane to advance and learn new seafaring skills. Here it is apparent because of the relatively short voyages undertaken by the *Millbay*, men like him were not so isolated from other social groups unlike those sailors working in bigger ships who as a consequence were compelled to undertake longer voyages.

Fig 12 .
Ketch "Millbay" alongside

As illustrated above, this type of vessel had two masts similar to that referred to by Fitzpatrick in *Sailing Ships of Mourne* wherein he points out that the one in the fore part, the mainmast, was the taller of the two. The second in the aft position was known as the mizzen, and from each of these two masts gaff and boom sails were set. Above the mainsail a gaff top-sail, jib headed is set (Fitzpatrick 32). Likewise above the mizzen a topsail is also visible, although Slade points out that some ketches, especially when they had been fitted with auxiliary diesel engines, had a tall main mast in one piece. Therefore the *Millbay's* rig appears to bear out his further assertion that in the days of relative prosperity before the First World War, a top sail was also set on the mizzen (Slade 17):

In drawing a contrast between this type of rig with that of the enormous mainsail of a cutter Conrad believes at anchor the former looks better. As he puts it "she has an aspect of greater efficiency and a better balance to the eye, with her two masts distributed over the hull with a swaggering rake aft" (qtd. in Conrad 39).

A brief look at the area north and south of the Irish Sea in which the *Millbay* traded shows that the eastern coast of Ireland is separated from Britain by relatively narrow channels, with the North channel between Ireland and Scotland only 13 miles across at its narrowest point. In the south at Wexford, for example, it is only 50 miles across to the coast of Wales another area frequently exporting coal to Ireland (Appendix D).

A - Main Sail	F - Bowsprit and Jib Boom	I - Mizzen Boom
B - Main Gaff Top-Sail	G - Sheets of 3 Foresails	J - Mizzen Sheet
C - Mizzen Sail	H - Main Boom – just forward	K - Main Top-sail Yard
D - Mizzen Topsail	is the punt with galley	L - Mizzen Yard
E - Martin Gale	adjacent	

As Mannering asserts these enclosed waters with strong tides, are characterised by choppy short seas while the heavily indented western coast from Donegal to Cork, contain large bays, numerous offshore islands and long fjord-like sea loughs, a topography reflected in coastal areas of Scotland, south-west Wales and south-west England (Mannering 219).

It was in these waters between 1902 and 1913 that this vessel carried many and varied cargoes including coal, peat, granite, limestone, whiting, bricks, timber, crabs, herring, kelp, maize, oats and salt. She traded between Truro in Cornwall, the Bristol Channel and Mersey Ports, the Isle of Man, from ports along the south, east and west coast of Ireland and in her final years as a trading vessel over into the Firth of Clyde and Western Isles of Scotland (Appendix E).

The *Millbay* traded throughout the First World War in the hazardous waters of the Irish Sea. This was in an area where German submarine activity was particularly intense, the German Government having warned all shipping that they regarded the waters around Great Britain and Ireland as a war zone (Phelan 19). Although a greater percentage of losses at sea during this war appear to relate to submarine warfare there was nevertheless a substantial proportion of conventional ship casualties. An example of the extent of this and the consequent dangers encountered by mariners is seen by the destruction of some 9,412,000 tons of shipping between July 1 1914 and December 31 1918 (Larn 180). This meant that those ships that survived were operating at a premium, allowing a renewed interest in small sailing ships such as the *Millbay* because they offered an economically attractive means of marine transportation during this period, as well as freeing up other larger vessels for military operations. As the war continued the dangers for shipping was also aggravated by the need to extinguish shore beacons, civilian blackouts and dimmed lights aboard ships. One example of the *Millbay's* involvement in hazardous wartime activities is reflected by an entry in the log-book in 1914 that records the transportation of 70 tons of dynamite from Irvine in western Scotland to Lamlash on the Isle of Arran (Appendix B). Added to this was the fact that this ship was often operating in a region of the Clyde critical to wartime operations. For example, Ardrossan brought orders for Admiralty vessels that included minesweepers as well as being a base for the repair and refitting of ships while further north on the Clyde estuary at Greenock, the Royal Navy's Torpedo Factory and Experiment and Design facilities were located (Osborne 87).

After the War and throughout the 1920's and 1930's the *Millbay* continued to work the Irish Sea trades. She carried coal into small harbours such as Teelin, Killybegs, Bruckless, Donegal Town, Mullaghmore in Co. Sligo and Ballina in Co. Mayo, returning with timber posts and kelp. Coastwise she carried oats from Killybegs and Letterkenny to Belmullet as well as timber into Teelin from Dublin. On occasions she carried scrap-iron from Killybegs, Bunbeg, Derry, Dublin and Belfast to Irvine in Scotland and carried peat from Burtonport and Buncrana to Campbeltown in Scotland (Appendix B).

With the approach of a Second World War her log records her arrival in Teelin with 95 tons of house coal from Troon in Scotland, and on the return voyage to the Clyde she carried 82 tons of scrap-iron from Killybegs. In June 1939 she carried 99 tons of coal to Donegal Town and then sailed to Ballina to load 40 tons of dried seaweed for Campbeltown. In August of the same year she was back in Killybegs with 100 tons of coal and on the morning of August 28th 1939, just days before the outbreak of World War II, her log records her last voyage from a Donegal port when she sailed in ballast for the Clyde.

While the official tonnage of shipping lost due to enemy action between September 3 1939 and September 2 1945 does not identify specific areas however it is on record that during World War II the Merchant Navy lost some 4,786 ships (Larn 190). It was in this period from September 1939 until August 1944 that the *Millbay* was seconded by the Admiralty and traded on the Scottish coast from Irvine and Troon out to Campbeltown in Kintyre, to the Arran ports, to Ardrishaig and northwards to Inveraray. On one particular voyage in 1941 her log records her carrying a cargo of gelignite and detonators for Loch Strivan and Belfast, returning to the Clyde with limestone from Carnlough (Appendix B).

Fig. 13.
Millbay at anchor Carnlough Harbour
Picture courtesy M.McCaughan, Ulster Folk & Transport Museum

From 1940 the western beaches of Scotland were used by British, American and other Allied forces to rehearse landing-craft techniques that included undercover units such as the Combined Operations Training Centre bases at Inveraray on Loch Fyne. It was in these waters that commando raids such as the one on the Norwegian Lofoten Islands in March 1941 were planned. The beaches of Ayrshire therefore were commandeered for the training of specialist forces that would equip them for the Torch amphibious landings later on in North Africa and the Husky invasion of Sicily (Osborne 144). These exercises therefore could be interpreted as a dress rehearsal for the D-Day Normandy landings later on in 1944. The vicinity of Ardrossan was once again witnessing considerable wartime activity having been taken over by the Admiralty and named *HMS Fortitude* (Osborne 87). Therefore because of the sensitivity surrounding such naval activities in this region, it was crucial as had been the case during World War I, that the extinguishing of navigational beacons and shore lights became a necessary precaution especially around the coast (Larn 191). Once again these wartime restrictions added to the peril of merchant trading vessels navigating these waters during this time. Despite the danger and disadvantages of wartime operations this ketch nevertheless continued a regular trade around the western coast of Scotland that included sensitive military areas such as Loch Fyne, the Isle of Bute, Kintyre and the Firth of Clyde. (Appendix E).

However as can be discerned from the log from around 1942 onwards this vessel appears to have been sailing more frequently "in ballast" between destinations (Appendix B). This points to diminishing cargo opportunities especially on her return voyages around this coast, and consequently it must be concluded that from then onwards the *Millbay* was operating at a loss. This pattern continued without interruption until 1944 when the log abruptly ends on August 2 of that year, where the last entry records that she sailed "in ballast" from the Clyde for Sharpness on the Severn Estuary which was to be her last voyage as a trading vessel:

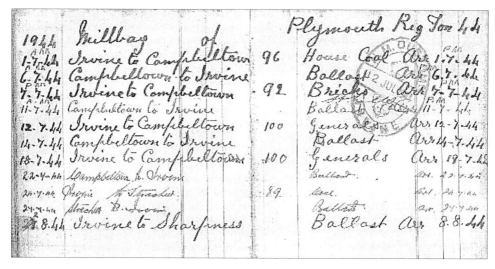

Fig. 14.
Last entry in Cargo Book 8 August 1944

Thus ended the *Millbay's* participation in a mercantile trade carried out between Great Britain and Ireland that involved her having had a trading contact with some 108 ports overall between 1902 until 1944 (Appendix E).

Fig. 15.
Barry Dock
Barry & District Photographic Memories:
Black Horse Books Telfont Salisbury.

The following extract of a letter written in 1944 from Douglas Hooper her new owner, to Johnny Chesnutt provides an insight into the navigational skills needed to negotiate the voyage from Barry Dock in south Wales up the River Severn (Appendix G) to the vessel's final destination at Upton:

New Theatre Buildings,   21ˢᵗ July 1944
Ross-on-Wye,
Herefordshire.
Ross-on-Wye.333/4

Dear Captain Chesnutt,

I have now heard from the Ministry that the transfer of your vessel *Millbay* to me has been sanctioned, and I would like to take this opportunity of expressing the appreciation of my wife and myself for the ready way in which you have met many requests and the pleasant atmosphere in which the transactions have been conducted.

I want to say that my very brief examination of the vessel showed me that you and your family had cared for her in a way that only seamen can, and now that she is going into honourable retirement, you can be sure that she will receive the same attention from us. If you know of anything which you think might be helpful to us in connection with her seaworthy qualities or her rig, I would be glad if you would kindly set it down for me, as you can imagine it will save time in the alterations we have to do.

I have made a small 2 ft. model of the vessel from memory, which I am particularly anxious for you to see when you get to Upton. I expect it is a good deal out, but the general principles are there. Actually I did not ask for the proper measurements from you, and I did not like to write a second time about them.

With regard to the voyage down, I will arrange with Thos. McLaren & Co. to cover insurance as soon as the Bill of Sale is through and the boat is at our disposal, and I would be glad if you would keep me in touch with a short telegram at each port you touch on the way down, so that I can fix my time to meet you on the way.

As you will ascertain, it will be necessary for you to put in to Barry and report to the Senior Naval Officer there. My wife and I had proposed to join you at Barry and do the last stage of the voyage with you, but as women are not allowed in Barry Dock, we would like you to pick us up, if you can, at either Minehead, Watchet or Weston Super Mare. Actually the best place would be Weston. We can probably get some local people to take us out to you, so if you will be good enough to wire me when you leave Barry, where you will have to take on a pilot, and about what time you are likely to arrive at Weston, we will arrange to be there at that time.

The voyage from Barry to Portishead is very tricky and there is a tremendous amount of shoal water, and you will certainly need a pilot, and if I were you, I would take him all the way up to Sharpness, because at Sharpness, unless you get right at the top of the flood, there is a very heavy current and getting in the lock entrance is just a headache.

From Sharpness to Gloucester there is 16 miles of canal, rather narrow, and again I think you would probably like to have a pilot At Gloucester we have to get the masts out of her, and then it is an easy day's journey as far as Upton, through two locks, with the channel shifting from port to starboard all the way up. The channel of the Severn between Gloucester and Upton varies between 10 ft. and 17 ft. and at her moorings the vessel will lie in about 10 ft. of water, summer level.

We shall need a bower anchor on a long scope of chain, also a kedge anchor, a head fast and stern fast and fore and aft springs. This may seem an unnecessary complication to you, but we have tankers going up and down the Severn, which draw quite a lot and suck the water up, so that boats on moorings surge up and down river, and most efficient moorings are necessary to prevent damage.

I hope you will not think me presumptuous in mentioning these things, in view of your lifelong experience of the sea, but I am sure that, as a seaman, you would like to know the local conditions as far as I can give them to you.

I certainly hope it will be possible for you to pick us up at Weston, but if it is inconvenient at all, please leave us out of the picture, as we do not want to interfere with your voyage in any way, but, as you can imagine, we should very much like to do the rest of the trip with you.

With kind regards,
Yours truly,
Douglas A. Hooper.

Fig 16.
Gloucester Dock and The Mariners' Church
Courtesy Carol Shayle

Thus the withdrawal of the *Millbay of Plymouth* from a coastal trade that spanned almost half a century produces a poignancy that could well echo Conrad's evocative description of a ship leaving her home port:

> The taking of Departure, if not the last sight of the land,
> is, perhaps, the last professional recognition of the land
> on the part of a sailor. It is the technical, as
> distinguished from the sentimental, "good-bye".
>
> Henceforth he has done with the coast astern of his
> ship. It is a matter personal to the man. (Conrad 2).

Therefore the success with which this vessel operated depended on the number of paying cargoes, otherwise her various owners could not maintain this trade. The size and facilities of the harbours also dictated the suitability of a ship such as this to load and unload successfully with the result that in many of the trading operations with which she was associated she had the edge on steam powered vessels because a steam-ship could not compete due to the smallness of the cargoes carried out at the behest of small business contractors. This was advantageous for sailing ships when compared to the high overheads associated with steamers where such port facilities would have rendered it uneconomical for them to accept the low freights offered in many remote regions. From an expertise perspective the skills involved in operating this ketch demonstrates that the sailors working on her were carrying on a tradition handed down by generations versed in techniques essential in handling and maintaining a profitable sailing vessel. It is also apparent that in the case of the *Millbay* both master and crew learned such skills through example as young men helping their fathers. Conversely, however, rail, road transport and improved technology was advancing steadily and many of these skills were gradually becoming obsolete because the environment which generated them could no longer be reproduced. Advances in shipbuilding led to the replacement of timber with iron and steel; steam propulsion also made it possible to introduce a more speedy and reliable form of sea trade. This meant arrival and departure dates could be advantageously gauged and these benefits were detrimental to small coastal traders coping with disadvantages such as the unpredictable dependency on weather conditions governing sail. The transport revolution that was evolving could be equated in a traditional Irish context to those changes that led to the factory and large-scale manufacturers replacing the handloom and craft weavers. Although most of the trades with which a small vessel such as the *Millbay* operated was soon overtaken by this general development of commerce, nevertheless as her log reflects, it could be argued ships of this size operating in small and isolated regions carried out a consistent trade in the teeth of mounting competition, allowed them considerable independence if not dominance in many of the coasting and short sea routes around Ireland and Great Britain during the first half of the twentieth century. A further analysis of this argument reveals that the longevity of the steamship was brief when measured against the life of the sailing ship having had a history that spanned many centuries of marine endeavour. What is not in doubt also is the evidence presented by this ketch's former crew-member that in working a ship of this size everyone on board from the master down co-operated because they all faced the elements together. This therefore appears to have been the case aboard the *Millbay of Plymouth.* From early in the century when she was involved in the Mourne trade, moving later to a more remote base in western Ireland and latterly trading amidst hazardous wartime conditions some forty years on, her log is testament to a life of tenacity and endeavour if lacking the application of speed. It is therefore still apparent as the present-day recollections illustrate that a lasting affinity generated by their shared experiences existed between this ship and the resilient men who sailed in her.

Work Cited

Bardon, Jonathan. *A Shorter Illustrated History of Ulster.* Belfast: The Blackstaff Press Limited, 1996.

Cannon, Brigid. Personal Interview, Portachran Kilcar 3rd October 2004.

Chesnutt, Hugh T. Personal Interview, Derrylaghan, Kilcar 3rd October 2004.

Conaghan, Pat. *The Zulu Fishermen – Forgotten Pioneers of Donegal's First Fishing Industry.* Killybegs: Bygones Enterprise, 2003.

Conrad, Joseph. *The Mirror of the Sea – Memories and Impressions.* London: Methuen & Co. 1906.

Cunningham, Catherine. Personal Interview, Kille, Kilcar 13th February 2005.

Cunningham, Moira. Personal Interview, Claddaghnageera, Kilcar 3rd October 2004.

Doyle, Gerry. Personal Interview, Moor Road, Kilkeel, 22nd November 2004.

Eglinton, Edmund. *The Last of the Sailing Coasters.* London: HMSO 1982.

Fitzpatrick, W.J. *Sailing Ships of Mourne.* Newcastle (Co. Down): Mourne Observer, 1971.

Greenhill, Basil. *The Merchant Schooners, Vol. 1.* London: Conway Maritime Press Ltd. 1988.

−//−. *The Ship – The Life and Death of the Merchant Sailing Ship 1815-1965* London: Her Majesty's Stationery Office, 1980.

Greenhill, Basil and Ann Giffard. *Victorian and Edwardian Ships and Harbours.* London: B.T. Batsford, 1978.

Larn, Richard. *Shipwrecks of Great Britain & Ireland.* Newton Abbot: David & Charles (Publishers) Ltd. 1981.

Latham, Tim. *The Ashburner Schooners – The Story of the First Shipbuilders of Barrow - In-Furness.* Manchester: Ready Rhino Publications, 1991.

Mannering, Julian. *The Chatham Directory of Inshore Craft – Traditional Working Vessels of the British Isles –* London: Chatham Publishing, 1997.

McBride, Elizabeth. Personal Interview, Harbour Road, Annalong, 23rd November 2004.

McCarthy, Charles. "Re: Millbay" E-mail to the author 24 October 2004.

McCaughan, Michael. *Sailing the Seaways – Historic maritime photographs from the Ulster Folk and Transport Museum 1864-1939.* Belfast: Friar's Bush Press, 1991.

McGeown, Mary. Personal Interview, Kilcar, 4th March 2005.

McShane, Michael. Personal Interview, Cloghan, Brockagh, Ballybofey, 23rd October 2004.

Osborne, Brian D. and Ronald Armstrong. *The Clyde at War.* Edinburgh: Birlinn Limited, 2001.

Phelan, Andrew. *Ireland from the Sea.* Dublin: Wolfhouse Press Ltd. 1998.

Slade, W.J. and Basil Greenhill. *Westcountry Coasting Ketches.* London: Conway Maritime Press, 1974.

Shayle, Carol. Original Photograph *The Mariners' Church, Gloucester Docks.* Printed by New Prospectives.

Appendices

Appendix A

Plymouth Millbay Dock, where the ketch *Millbay* was built located in the "Shipbuilding" shed on the north-west corner.

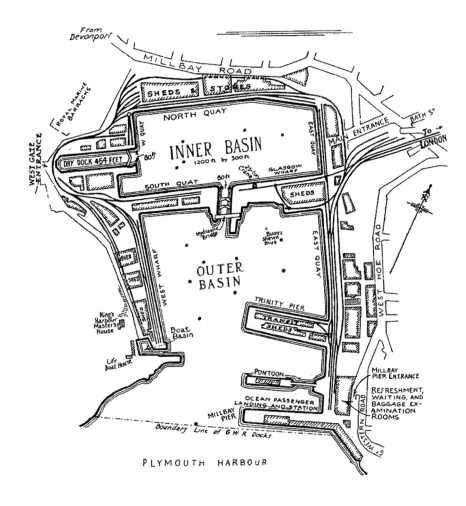

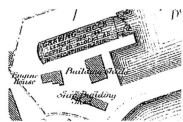

Courtesy Plymouth City Museum & Art Gallery.

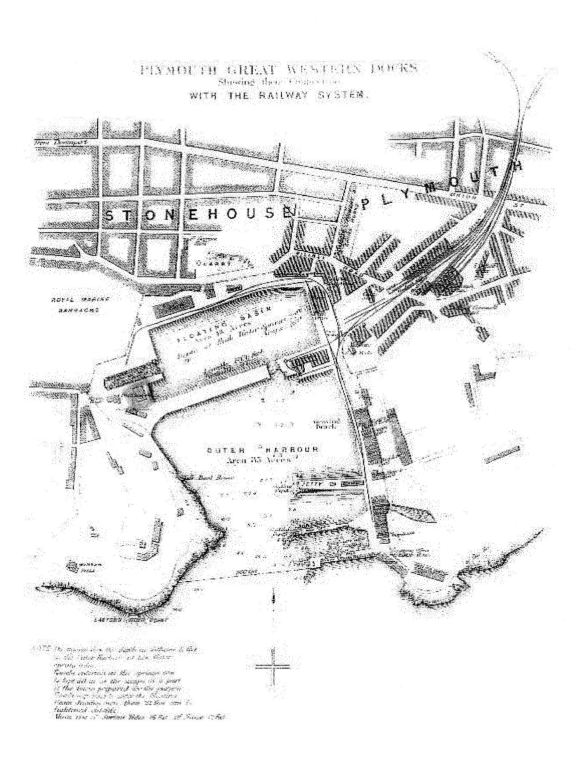

PLYMOUTH GREAT WESTERN DOCKS
Showing their Connection
WITH THE RAILWAY SYSTEM.

Appendix B

Cargo Log of Millbay of Plymouth 1902-44

Year	Destination	Cargo	Duration of Voyage
1902	Maryport to Kilkeel	Coal	November 5 1902
	Kilkeel to Newport	Potatoes	December 22 1902
1903	Newport to Wexford	Crabs	Left January 12 Arr. January 14
	Wexford to Kilkeel	Ballast	Left January 22 Arr. January 23
	Kilkeel to Bristol	Potatoes	Left Kilkeel February 3 Arr. Bristol February 15
	Bristol to Newport	Light	Left Bristol February 28 Arr. same day
	Newport to Whitegate	Crabs	Left Newport April 20 Arr. Whitegate April 22
	Whitegate to Garston	Timber	Left May 7 Arr. May 16 1903
	Garston to Rostrevor	100 tons Coal	Arrived May 25 03
	Rostrevor to Annalong	Light	
	Annalong to Liverpool	105 tons Kerbs	Arrived June 12
	Liverpool and Ellesmere Pt. to Dalbeattie	Coke and Guams	June 20
	Dalbeattie to Workington	Ballast	June 30
	Workington to Kilkeel	100 tons Coal	July 9
	Kilkeel to Annalong	Light	July 20
	Annalong to Liverpool	100 tons Kerbs	Arrived July 20 1903
	Garston to Annalong	100 tons Coal	Left Liverpool August 5
	Annalong to Garston	Setts & Kerbs	Arrived September 2
	Garston to Kilkeel	100 tons Coal	Left L/pool ?
	Kilkeel to Annalong	Light	
	Annalong to Belfast	100 Tons Granite Setts	
	Belfast to Workington	62 1/2 tons Scrap Iron	
	Workington to Annalong	100 tons Coal	
	Annalong to Belfast	100 tons Granite	
1904	Belfast to Newross	101 tons Maize	January 20 1904
	Newross to Swansea	66 tons Oats	February 4 1904
	Swansea to Dublin	105 tons Coal	

	Dublin to Kilkeel	40 tons Manure	
	Kilkeel to Neath	85 tons Potatoes	
	Neath to Wexford	105 tons Coal	April 12 1904
	Wexford to Kilkeel	Ballast	April 25 1904
	Kilkeel to Annalong	-	May 9
	Annalong to Kilkeel	Granite blocks, etc.	May 15
	Workington to Annalong	100 tons Coal	May 18
	Annalong to Liverpool	105 tons Stone	May 20
	Liverpool to Strangford	105 tons Coal	L/pool June 30 1904
	Strangord to Annalong	Light	
	Annalong to Garston	105 tons Kerbs	L/pool July 24 04
	Garston to Kilkeel	100 tons Coal	Do July 30 04
	Kilkeel to Garston	105 tons Kerbs	Do 9.9.04
	Garston to Kilkeel	100 tons Coal	Do 15.9.04
	Kilkeel to Annalong	Light	
	Annalong to Liverpool	100 tons Kerbs	L/pool 10.04
	Liverpool to Rostrevor	100 tons Coal	Do 10.04
	Rostrevor to Bristol	95 tons Potatoes	31.12.04
1905	Bristol to Kilkeel	40 tons Coal	January 17 1905
	Kilkeel to Cardiff	95 tons Potatoes	February 4
	Cardiff to Waterford	105 tons Coal	March 3
	Waterford to Garston	60 tons Timber	March 27 Arrived April 1
	Garston to Rostrevor	100 tons Coal	April 7
	Rostrevor to Kilkeel	Light	April 16
	Kilkeel to Swansea	90 tons Potatoes	May 8
	Swansea to Dublin	105 tons Coal	
	Dublin to Glasgow	105 tons Timber	June 1
	Glasgow to Mullaghmore	95t.12c. Coal	Left Glasgow June 16 Arr. M. More June 30
	Mullaghmore to Bowling	105 tons Kelp	July 6
	Bowling to Llanelly	95 tons Steel Stavings	July 22 Arr. July 05
	Llanelly to Wexford	105 tons Steam Coal	Aug. 4 Arr. Aug. 24
	Wexford to Kilkeel	Ballast	Arrived September 6
	Kilkeel to Cardiff	90 tons Potatoes	Left Nov. 1 Arrived Nov. 8
	Cardiff to Kilkeel	100 tons Steam Coal H. Silcocks	Arrived November 10

1906	Kilkeel to Neath	100 tons Potatoes	January 3 Arrived January 18
	Neath to Arklow	109 tons Coal	Arrived January 21
	Arklow to Garston	100 tons Nitre Cake	Arrived February 20
	Garston to Kilkeel	110 tons Coal	Left March 1 Arrived March 7
	Kilkeel to Garston	100 tons Setts	Arrived March 30
	Garston to Rostrevor	105 tons Coal	Left April 6 Arrived April 20
	Rostrevor to Kilkeel	Light	
	Kilkeel to Manchester	90 tons Potatoes	Arrived May 14
	Manchester to Castleward	100 tons Coal House & Lancs.	Arrived May 25
		Light	
	Castleward to Workington	110 tons Coal	Arrived June 14
	Workington to Kilkeel	110 tons Setts	Arrived July 7
	Kilkeel to Garston	100 tons Coal	
	Garston to Giles Quay	Light	
	Giles Quay to Dundalk	107 tons Scrap Iron	Left August 1
	Dundalk to Workington	96 tons Coal	Left August 18 Arrived August 23
	Workington to Clogherhead		
	Note: Cargo boats to show the place of origin and description of coal		
	Clogherhead to Warrenpoint	Ballast	Left August 23 Arrived August 28
	Warrenpoint to Kilkeel	Ballast	October 18
	Kilkeel to Cardiff	90 tons Potatoes	Left November 18 Arrived November 29
	Cardiff to Ballinacurra	98 tons Coal	Arrived December 22
1907	Ballinacurra to Truro	-	Left January 7 Arrived January 15
	Truro to Penrhyn	Light	
	Penrhyn to Swansea	Granite Blocks	
	Swansea to Dublin	Coal	
	Annalong to Gloucester	Potatoes	
	Gloucester to New Ross	Salt	
	New Ross to Bridgewater	870 Brls Oats	
	Bridgewater to Waterford	100 tons Brickyard Goods	
	Waterford to Port Talbot	100 tons Timber	
	Port Talbot to Bangor	Coal	

	Bangor to Belfast	Bales	Arrived July 18
	Belfast to Llanelly	104 tons Steel	
	Llanelly to Dublin	103 tons Large House Coal	
	Dublin to Workington	100 tons Scrap Iron	
	Workington to Wexford	100 tons House Coal	Left October 1 Arrived October 7
	Wexford to Kilkeel	Ballast	Left October 15 do October 26
	Kilkeel to Pembroke Dock	Potatoes	Left November 21 do November 28
	Pembroke Dock to Glasgow	Bricks	December 1
1908	Glasgow to Cork	Manures & Seeds in Bags	January 23
	Cork to Garston	70 tons Timber	
	Garston to Kilkeel	100 tons Coal	C.H. Liverpool April 16 1908
	Kilkeel to Annalong	Light	
	Annalong to Liverpool	100 tons Stone	C.H. Liverpool May 20 1908
	Liverpool to Garston	Light	
	Garston to Omeath Beach	105 tons Coal	C.H. Liverpool May 28 1908
	Omeath Beach to Annalong	Light	
	Annalong to Liverpool	100 tons Kerbs	Arrived June 13 1908
	Liverpool to Garston	Light	
	Garston to Quoile Quay	105 tons Coal	C.H. Liverpool June 20 1908
	Quoile Quay to Maryport	Light	July 15 1908
	Maryport to Clougher Head	Coals	Left July 21 Arrived July 27 1908
	Clougher Head to Kilkeel	Light	August 1 1908
	Kilkeel to Milford-Haven	Potatoes	Left November 29 Arrived December 6 1908
	Note: The place of origin and description of any coal carried as cargo are required to be given in Cargo Book by Customs in future (GO 13/1906) Geo Clark, Colls. 3 Mch 1909.		
1909	Milford-Haven to Kilkeel	Light	Left December 31 1908 Arrived January 5 1909
	Kilkeel to Llanelly	92 tons Potatoes	Left February 23 Arrived February 27
	Llanelly to Campbeltown	105 tons Large Anthracite Coal	Left March 16 Arrived April 8

	Campbeltown to Belfast	100 tons Dross	April 21
	Cap. J. Doyle April 30		
	Belfast to Kilkeel	100 tons General Cargo	May 6
	Kilkeel to Annalong	Light	
	Annalong to Whitehaven	--	June 5
	Whitehaven to Kilkeel	100 tons Raw Coal	CCH September 3 1909
	Ballycotton to Milford	Potatoes	Arrived November 20 1909
	Whitehaven to Pembroke Dock	Part Cargo Potatoes	Arrived December 7 1909
	Balbriggan to Swansea	68 tons Steel Scrap	Arrived December 31
	Maryport to Kilkeel	(no entry in log)	
1910	Swansea to Dublin	100 tons Coal	Left January 22
	Dublin to Waterford	105 tons Manure	Left March 8 Arrived March 22
	Waterford to Ayr	80 tons Timber	Left April 1 Arrived April 22
	Ayr to Port William	105 tons Coal	Left May 9 Arrived May 10
	Port William to Whitehaven	Light	Arrived May 15
	Whitehaven to Skerries	105 tons House Coal	Arrived May 27 1910
	Skerries to Ramsey	Ballast	Left June 13 1910
	Ramsey to Garnish Bay	105 tons Salt	Left June 22 1910
	Garnish Bay to Maryport	Light	
	Maryport to Kilkeel	100 tons Coal	Left August 2 Arrived August 14
1911	Kilkeel to Liverpool	74 tons Potatoes	Left January 12 Arrived January 16
	Liverpool to Garston	Light	Left January 20 Arrived January 20
	Garston to Kilkeel	100 tons Coal	
	Kilkeel to Cardiff	75 tons Potatoes	Left February 17 Arrived March 14 1911
	Cardiff to Kilkeel	100 tons Coal	Left March 14 Arrived April 4
	Kilkeel to Annalong	Light	Left April 13 Arrived April 13
	Annalong to Cork	100 tons Granite Stone	Left April 14 Arrived May 2
	Cork to Garston	65 tons Timber	Left May 17 Arrived May 22
	Garston to Annalong	100 tons Coal	Left May 30
	Annalong to Cork	100 tons Granite Stone	Left June 14 Arrived June 18
	Cork to Garston	Timber	Left June 30

	Garston to Westonpoint	Light	Left July 12 1911
	Westonpoint to Girvan	105 tons Salt	Left July14 (H.M. Customs Girvan July 25 1911)
	Girvan to Maryport	Ballast	Left August 9 1911
	Maryport to Kilkeel	100 tons Coals	Left August 16
	Kilkeel to Annalong	Ballast	September 6
	Annalong to Ellesmere Port	100 tons Setts	Left September 7
	Ellesmere Port to Garston	Light	Left September 18 1911
	Garston to Kilkeel	105 tons House Coal	Left September 20
	Kilkeel to Maryport	Light	Left October 24
	Maryport to Kilkeel	101tons Large House Coal	Left November 7
	Kilkeel to Pembroke Dock	Potatoes	(no entry logged)
1912	Pembroke Dock to Swansea	Ballast	
	Swansea to Dublin	105 tons Coal	Left February 12 1912
	Dublin to Kilkeel	105 tons Manure	Left March 3 Arr. March 5
	Kilkeel to Pembroke Dock	95 tons Potatoes	Left March 22 Arr. March 29
	Pembroke Dock to Saundersfoot	100 tons Coal	Left May 15 Arr. May 16
	Saundersfoot to Drogheda	110 tons Coal	Left May 19 Arr. May 29
	Drogheda to Garston	93 tons Scrap Iron	Left June 12 Arr. June 14
	Garston to Omeath	100 tons House Coal	Left July 2 Arr. July 5
	Omeath to Ramsey	Light	Left July 13 Arr. July 15
	Ramsey to Courtown	105 tons Salt	Left July 22 Arr. July 29
	Courtown to Rostrevor	Light	Left August 5 Arr. August 6
	Rostrevor to Garston	70 tons Timber	Left August 15 Arr. August 20
	Garston to Rostrevor	105 tons Coal	Left August 26 Arr. September 14
	Rostrevor to Garston	(no entry in log)	Left October 3 Arr. October 5
	Garston to Kilkeel	101 Tons Coal	Left October 23 Arr. October 30
	Kilkeel to Belfast	91 tons Stones (setts) 5 tons Herrings	Left November 28 Arr. November 29
	Belfast to Irvine	100 tons Scrap Iron	Left December 10 Arr. December 23
		Half Yearly ending Dec.31	

1913	Irvine to Campbeltown	100 tons House Coal Montgomeryfield Colliery	Left January 7 Arr. January 10
	Campbeltown to Irvine	Ballast	Left February 12 Arr. February 14
	Irvine to Campbeltown	103 tons 7cwt. House Coal Montgomeryfield Colliery	Left February 21 Arr. February 21
	Irvine to Carnlough	106 tons House Coal Montgomeryfield Colliery	Left March 31 Arr. April 1
	Carnlough to Dublin	107 tons Whiting	Left April 8 Arr. April 9
	Dublin to Castletown and Ramsey	100 tons Manure	Left May 1 Arr. May 2
	Ramsey to Campbeltown and Irvine	106 tons 3 cwt. Salt	Left May 23 Arr. May 24
	Irvine to Teelin	100 tons House Coal Montgomeryfield Colliery	Left June 11 Arr. June 20
	Teelin to Mullaghmore	Ballast	Left July 2 Arr. July 2
	Mullaghmore to Bowling	108 tons 9cwt. Kelp	Left July 6 Arr. July 16
	Bowling to Greenock	Light (Half Year)	Left July 21
	Greenock to Burtonport	104 tons 1cwt. House Coal	Left July 24 Arr. July 26
	Burtonport to Irvine	81 tons Kelp	Left August 10 Arr. August 12
	Irvine to Carnlough	100 tons Montgomeryfield House Coal	Left August 19 Arr. August 21
	Carnlough to Dublin	105 tons Whiting	Left August 27 Arr. August 29
	Dublin to Irvine	102 Tons Purple Ore	Left September 8 Arr. September 11
	Irvine to Campbeltown	100 tons Corsehill House Coal	Left September 13 Arr. September 17
	Campbeltown to Irvine	Ballast	Left October 15 Arr. October 15
	Irvine to Campbeltown	100 tons Springside House Coal	Left October 23 Arr. October 23
	Campbeltown to Irvine	Ballast	Left November 4 Arr. November 4
	Irvine to Campbeltown	101 tons Springside House Coal	Left November 7 Arr. November 8
	Campbeltown to Irvine	Ballast	Left November 20 Arr. November 20
	Irvine to Campbeltown	100 tons Corsehill House Coal	Left December 5 Arr. December 5
	Campbeltown to Irvine	Ballast	Left December 13 Arr. December 13

	Irvine to Campbeltown	96 tons Springside House Coal	Left December 24 Arr. December 24
1914	Campbeltown to Irvine	Ballast	Left January 27 Arr. January 27
	Irvine to Campbeltown	103 tons Corsehill House Coal	Left February 10 Arr. February 10
	Campbeltown to Irvine	Ballast	Left February 23 Arr. February 23
	Irvine to Campbeltown	101 tons Corsehill House Coal	Left March 7 Arr. March 8
	Campbeltown to Irvine	Ballast	Left March 22 Arr. March 22
	Irvine to Carnlough	105 tons Montgomeryfield House Coal	Left March 24 Arr. March 27
	Carnlough to Dublin	105 tons Whiting	Left April 8 Arr. April 15
	Dublin to Castletown Note: Inspected at Castletown 9.4.1914 T.Hayes Offr.	(Part Cargo) Manure	Left May 6 Arr. May 7
	Castletown to Ramsey	With remainder of Manure	Left May 12 Arr. May 12
	Ramsey to Belmullet	103 Tons Salt	Left May 19 Arr. June 8
	Belmullet to Mullaghmore	Ballast	Left June 18 Arr. June 18
	Mullaghmore to Bowling	Kelp	Left June 25 Arr. June 30
	Bowling to Greenock	Ballast	Left July 9 Arr. July 9
	Greenock to Teelin	101 tons House Coal	Left July 12 Arr. July 15
	Teelin to Buncrana	Ballast	Left August 4 Arr. August 17
	Buncrana to Campbeltown	68 tons Peat	Left August 25 Arr. August 26
	Campbeltown to Irvine	Ballast	Left September 2 Arr. September 3
	Irvine to Donegal	101 tons Montgomeryfield Coal	Left September 8 Arr. October 7
	Donegal to Troon	Timber	Left October 17 Arr. October 20
	Troon to Campbeltown	100 tons Corsehill House Coal	Left October 27 Arr. October 29
	Campbeltrown to Ayr	Ballast	Left November 7 Arr. November 7
	Ayr to Campbeltown	104 tons Corsehill House Coal	Left November 16 Arr. November 16
	Campbeltown to Irvine	Ballast	Left December 29 Arr. December 29
	Irvine to Lamlash	70 tons Dinamite (dynamite)	Left December 31 Arr. December 31

1915	Lamlash to Irvine	Light	Left January 22 Arr. January 22
	Irvine to Campbeltown	101 tons Corsehill House Coal	Left January 23 Arr. January 24
	Campbeltown to Troon	Ballast	Left January 30 Arr. January 30
	Troon to Campbeltown	102 tons Corsehill House Coal	Left February 9 Arrived February 9
	Campbeltown to Troon	Ballast	Left February 20 Arr. February 20
	Troon to Campbeltown	102 tons Corsehill House Coal	Left February 26 Arr. March 7
	Campbeltown to Ayr	12 tons Manure	Left March 11 Arr. March 12
	Ayr to Campbeltown	103 tons Yanch House Coal	Left March 13 Arr. March 14
	Campbeltown to Ayr	Ballast	Left March 27 Arr. March 28
	Ayr to Campbeltown	102 tons Steam Coal – V Bairds	Left March 29 Arr. March 30
	Campbeltown to Troon	Ballast	Left April 10 Arr. April 10
	Troon to Campbeltown	103 tons Baracula Coal	Left April 12 Arr. April 14
	Campbeltown to Irvine	Ballast	Left April 21 Arr. April 21
	Irvine to Carnlough	105 Tons Ell Coal	Left April 28 Arr. April 29
	Carnlough to Dublin	106 Tons Whiting	Left May 7 Arr. May 8
	Dublin to Ardrossan	101 tons Purpleore	Left May 28 Arr. June 1
	Ardrossan to Campbeltown	90 tons Steam Coal	Left June 5 Arr. June 6
	Campbeltown to Irvine	Ballast	Left June 15 Arr. June 16
	Irvine to Campbeltown	103 tons Springside Coal	Left June 18 Arr. June 18
	Campbeltown to Ayr	Ballast	Left June 29 Arr. June 30
	Ayr to Campbeltown (Half Year)	103 tons Steam Coal Auchinoriure	Left July 1 Arr. July 2
	Campbeltown to Ardrossan	Ballast	Left July 9 Arr. July 9
	Ardrossan to Campbeltown	97 tons Steam Coal	Left July 14 Arr. July 15
	Campbeltown to Irvine	Ballast	Left July 21 Arr. July 21
	Irvine to Campbeltown	102 tons Steam Coal	Left July 24 Arr. July 25
	Campbeltown to Troon	Ballast	Left July 30 Arr. July 30
	Troon to Campbeltown	102 tons Fairlie Coal	Left August 4 Arr. August 5
	Campbeltown to Irvine	Ballast	Left August 16 Arr. August 16
	Irvine to Carnlough	104 tons Springside House Coal	Left August 18 Arr. August 19
	Carnlough to Dublin	107 Tons Whiting	Left August 26 Arr. August 29

	Dublin to Ardrossan	101 tons Purpleore	Left September 8 Arr. September 10
	Ardrossan to Campbeltown	100 tons Longregg House Coal	Left September 20 Arr. September 20
	Campbeltown to Ayr	--	Left October 12 Arr.October 12
	Ayr to Campbeltown	100 tons South Longregg & Drumsmudden Coal	Left October 15 Arr. October 16
	Campbeltown to Ayr	Ballast	Left October 26 Arr. October 27
	Ayr to Campbeltown	100 tons South Longregg Coal	Left November 3 Arr. November 3
	Campbeltown to Irvine	Ballast	Left November 16 Arr. November 17
	Irvine to Campbeltown	100 tons South Longregg Coal	Left November 20 Arr. November 20
	Campbeltown to Irvine	Ballast	Left December 2 Arr. December 3
	Irvine to Campbeltown	102 tons South Longregg Coal	Left December 17 Arr. December 17
1916	Campbeltown to Irvine	Ballast	Left January 14 Arr. January 14
	Irvine to Campbeltown	102 tons Corsehill House Coal	Left January 30 Arr. January 31
	Campbeltown to Irvine	Ballast	Left March 4 Arr. March 4
	Irvine to Campbeltown	101 tons Corsehill House Coal	Left March 14 Arr. March 14
	Campbeltown to Irvine	100 tons Sand	Left April 5 Arr. April 6
	Irvine to Carnlough	106 tons General	Left April 15 Arr. April 16
	Carnlough to Dublin	108 Tons Whiting	Left April 22 Arr. May 4
	Dublin to Irvine	103 tons Purple Ore	Left May 20 Arr. May 23
	Irvine to Campbeltown	103 tons Corsehill House Coal	Left May 29 Arr. May 29
	Campbeltown to Belfast	105 tons Steam Coal	Left June 14 Arr. June 15
	Belfast to Glasgow	105 tons Scrap Iron	Left June 21 Arr. June 26
	Glasgow to Campbeltown	100 tons House Coal Lanarkshire	Left July 8 Arr. July 9
		Half Year ended	
	Campbeltown to Irvine	Ballast	Left July 15 Arr. July 15
	Irvine to Carnlough	103 tons Corsehill House Coal	Left July 20 Arr. July 23
	Carnlough to Dublin	106 tons Whiting	Left July 28 Arr. July 31
	Dublin to Irvine	105 tons Purple Ore	Left August 10 Arr. August 12
	Irvine to Carnlough	105 tons Corsehill House Coal	Left August 16 Arr. August 17

	Carnlough to Dublin	105 tons Whiting	Left August 26 Arr. August 29
	Dublin to Irvine	104 tons Burned Ore	Left September 13 Arr. September 22
	Irvine to Campbeltown	102 tons Corsehill House Coal	Left September 28 Arr. September 29
	Campbeltown to Irvine	82 tons Sand	Left October 24 Arr. October 25
	Irvine to Campbeltown	101 tons Corsehill House Coal	Left October 28 Arr. October 29
	Campbeltown to Irvine	109 Tons Sand	Left November 22 Arr. November 22
	Irvine to Campbeltown	103 tons Corsehill House Coal	Left November 25 Arr. November 26
	Campbeltown to Irvine	105 tons Sand	Left December 4 Arr. December 4
	Irvine to Campbeltown	101 tons Corsehill House Coal	Left December 8 Arr. December 9
		Half Year Ended	
	Campbeltown to Irvine	Ballast	Left February 2 Arr. February 2
1917	Irvine to Campbeltown	103 tons Corsehill House Coal	Left February 9 Arr. February 9
	Campbeltown to Irvine	100 tons Sand	Left February 22 Arr. February 22
	Irvine to Campbeltown	105 tons Corsehill House Coal	Left March 1 Arr. March 1
	Campbeltown to Irvine	66 tons Sand	Left March 22 Arr. March 22
	Irvine to Carnlough	104 tons Slack & House, Springside	Left March 31 Arr. April 8
	Carnlough to Dublin	105 tons Whiting	Left April 20 Arr. April 23
	Dublin to Ardrossan	104 tons Burned Ore	Left May 14 Arr. May 23
	Ardrossan to Campbeltown	101 ton Steam Coal	Left May 29 Arr. May 30
	Campbeltown to Irvine	105 tons Sand	Left June 3 Arr. June 5
	Irvine to Campbeltown	106 tons Steam Coal	Left June 7 Arr. June 8
	Campbeltown to Irvine	100 tons Sand	Left June 19 Arr. June 20
	Irvine to Campbeltown	106 tons Steam Coal	Left June 25 Arr. June 25
	Campbeltown to Irvine	102 tons Sand	Left June 29 Arr. July 1
		Half Year 1917	
	Irvine to Campbeltown	101 tons Jewel Coal	Left July 3 Arr. July 4
	Campbeltown to Irvine	104 tons Sand	Left July 19 Arr. July 20
	Irvine to Campbeltown	103 tons Jewel Coal	Left July 27 Arr. July 28
	Campbeltown to Irvine	98 tons Sand	Left August 11 Arr. August 12
	Irvine to Campbeltown	105 tons Jewel Coal	Left August 16 Arr. August 17
	Campbeltown to Irvine	101 tons Sand	Left August 31 Arr. August 31

	Irvine to Campbeltown	104 tons Jewel Coal	Left September 5 Arr. September 6
	Campbeltown to Irvine	100 tons Sand	Left September 18 Arr. September 18
	Irvine to Campbeltown	140 tons Steam Coal	Left October 10 Arr. October 10
	Campbeltown to Irvine	100 tons Sand	Left October 18 Arr. October 18
	Irvine to Campbeltown	100 tons Steam Coal	Left October 29 Arr. October 31
	Campbeltown to Irvine	105 tons Sand	Left November 13 Arr. November 14
	Irvine to Campbeltown	103 tons Jewel Coal	Left November 20 Arr. November 21
	Campbeltown to Irvine	95 tons Sand	Left December 6 Arr. December 8
	Irvine to Campbeltown	100 tons Jewel Coal	Left December 17 Arr. December 17
		First of Half Year 1918	
1918	Campbeltown to Troon	104 tons Sand	Left February 11 Arr. February 11
	Troon to Campbeltown	101 tons House Coal	Left February 17 Arr. February 18
	Campbeltown to Irvine	102 tons Sand	Left March 12 Arr. March 13
	Irvine to Belfast	102 tons Steam Coal	Left March 23 Arr. March 25
	Belfast to Irvine	104 tons Scrap Iron	Left April 5 Arr. April 6
	Irvine to Belfast	104 tons Steam Coal	Left April 13 Arr. April 14
	Belfast to Irvine	103 tons Scrap Iron	Left April 22 Arr. April 23
	Irvine to Belfast	104 tons Steam Coal	Left May 7 Arr. May 8
	Belfast to Irvine	105 tons Scrap Iron	Left May 25 Arr. May 28
	Irvine to Carnlough	102 tons House Coal	Left June 11 Arr. June 12
	Carnlough to Dublin	108 tons Whiting	Left June 24 Arr. June 25
		Half Year	
	Dublin to Irvine	100 tons Scrap Iron	Left July 12 Arr. July 14
	Irvine to Dublin	104 tons House Coal	Left August 9 Arr. August 16
	Dublin to Irvine	100 tons Scrap Iron	Left August 24 Arr. August 31
	Irvine to Campbeltown	100 tons House Coal	Left September 7 Arr. September 8
	Campbeltown to Belfast	95 tons House Coal	Left September 29 Arr. September 30
	Belfast to Glasgow	101 tons Scrap Iron	Left October 11 Arr. October 14
	Glasgow to Campbeltown	100 tons Coal	Left October 21 Arr. October 24
	Campbeltown to Troon	61 tons Scrap Iron	Left November 11 Arr. November 11
	Troon to Campbeltown	106 tons House Coal	Left November 19 Arr. November 19

	Campbeltown to Belfast	99 tons House Coal Half Year	Left November 29 Arr. November 30
1919	Belfast to Irvine	100 tons Scrap Iron	Left January 11 Arr. January 12
	Irvine to Campbeltown	104 tons House Coal	Left January 18 Arr. January 19
	Campbeltown to Belfast	103 tons House Coal	Left January 28 Arr. January 28
	Belfast to Irvine	105 tons Scrap Iron	Left March 16 Arr. March 17
	Irvine to Campbeltown	101 tons House Coal	Left March 25 Arr. March 26
	Campbeltown to Belfast	101 tons House Coal	Left April 3 Arr. April 4
	Belfast to Irvine	104 tons Scrap Iron	Left April 12 Arr. April 13
	Irvine to Campbeltown	101 tons House Coal	Left April 18 Arr. April 19
	Campbeltown to Belfast	102 tons House Coal	Left April 24 Arr. Apr. 25
	Belfast to Irvine	105 tons Scrap Iron	Left May 10 Arr. May 11
	Irvine to Campbeltown	106 tons House Coal	Left May 17 Arr. May 18
	Campbeltown to Irvine	100 tons Sand	Left May 27 Arr. May 28
	Irvine to Campbeltown	102 tons House Coal	Left May 31 Arr. June 1
	Campbeltown to Belfast	100 tons House Coal	Left June 18 Arr. June 18
	Belfast to Irvine	103 tons Scrap Iron	Left June 27 Arr. June 28
	Irvine to Belfast	100 tons Bricks	Left July 7 Arr. July 8
	Belfast to Irvine	105 tons Scrap Iron	Left July 31 Arr. August 1
	Irvine to Derry	101 tons Coal	Left August 14 Arr. August 17
	Derry to Irvine	105 tons Scrap Iron	Left August 31 Arr. September 2
	Irvine to Campbeltown	104 tons House Coal	Left September 11 Arr. September 11
	Campbeltown to Belfast	101 tons House Coal	Left September 27 Arr. September 27
	Belfast to Irvine	100 tons Scrap Iron	Left October 4 Arr. October 5
	Irvine to Campbeltown	101 tons House Coal	Left October 14 Arr. October 14
	Campbeltown to Belfast	100 tons Coal	Left November 1 Arr. November 2
	Belfast to Irvine	102 tons Scrap iron	Left December 1 Arr. December 7
	Irvine to Campbeltown	106 tons House Coal	Left December 25 Arr. December 26
1920	Campbeltown to Irvine	Ballast	Left February 4 Arr. February 4
	Irvine to Campbeltown	102 tons House Coal	Left February 14 Arr. February 14
	Campbeltown to Irvine	Ballast	Left February 21 Arr. February 21
	Irvine to Campbeltown	109 Tons House Coal	Left February 25 Arr. February 25
	Campbeltown to Irvine	Ballast	Left March 5 Arr. March 5
	Irvine to Campbeltown	105 tons House Coal	Left March 11 Arr. March 11

	Campbeltown to Irvine	Ballast	Left March 30 Arr. April 4
	Irvine to Campbeltown	107 tons House Coal	Left April 9 Arr. April 9
	Campbeltown to Irvine	Ballast	Left April 23 Arr. April 23
	Irvine to Belfast	105 tons Fireclay	Left May 10 Arr. May 11
	Belfast to Irvine	105 tons Scrap Iron	Left May 28 Arr. May 31
	Irvine to Dublin	100 tons House Coal	Left June 8 Arr. June 24
		Half Year	
	Dublin to Irvine	105 tons Scrap Iron	Left July 9 Arr. July 10
	Irvine to Campbeltown	104 tons House Coal	Left August 4 Arr. August 5
	Campbeltown to Irvine	Ballast	Left August 11 Arr. August 11
	Irvine to Campbeltown	105 tons House Coal	Left August 12 Arr. August 13
	Campbeltown to Irvine	Ballast	Left August 21 Arr. August 21
	Irvine to Campbeltown	103 tons House Coal	Left August 24 Arr. August 25
	Campbeltown to Irvine	Ballast	Left August 28 Arr. August 28
	Irvine to Campbeltown	103 tons House Coal	Left September 7 Arr. September 7
	Campbeltown to Irvine	Ballast	Left September 13 Arr. September 13
	Irvine to Campbeltown	108 tons House Coal	Left September 16 Arr. September 16
	Campbeltown to Irvine	Ballast	Left November 5 Arr. November 5
	Irvine to Kircubbin	105 tons House Coal	Left November 22 Arr. November 29
1921	Kircubbin to Belfast	Light	Left January 25 Arr. January 27
	Belfast to Irvine	104 tons Scrap Iron	Left February 13 Arr. February 19
	Irvine to Campbeltown	103 tons House Coal	Left March 5 Arr. March 6
	Campbeltown to Irvine	Ballast	Left March 19 Arr. March 19
	Irvine to Campbeltown	103 tons House Coal	Left March 25 Arr. March 26
	Campbeltown to Irvine	Ballast	Left March 31 Arr. March 31
	Irvine to Campbeltown	102 tons House Coal	Left April 7 Arr. April 8
	Campbeltown to Irvine	Ballast	Left June 30 Arr. July 1
		Half Year	
	Irvine to Campbeltown	102 tons House Coal	Left July 14 Arr. July 15
	Campbeltown to Irvine	Ballast	Left July 25 Arr. July 25
	Irvine to Campbeltown	106 tons House Coal	Left July 28 Arr. July 28
	Campbeltown to Irvine	Ballast	Left August 6 Arr. August 6
	Irvine to Campbeltown	105 tons House Coal & Tiles	Left August 11 Arr. August 11

	Campbeltown to Irvine	Ballast	Left August 23 Arr. August 23
	Irvine to Campbeltown	109 tons House Coal	Left August 25 Arr. August 25
	Campbeltown to Irvine	Ballast	Left September 2 Arr. September 2
	Irvine to Campbeltown	101 tons House Coal	Left September 20 Arr. September 20
	Irvine to Campbeltown	103 tons House Coal	Left September 23 Arr. September 24
	Campbeltown to Irvine	Ballast	Left October 7 Arr. October 7
	Irvine to Campbeltown	105 tons House Coal	Left October 11 Arr. October 11
	Campbeltown to Irvine	Ballast	Left October 15 Arr. October 15
	Irvine to Campbeltown	105 tons House Coal	Left October 22 Arr. October 23
	Campbeltown to Irvine	Ballast	Left October 30 Arr. October 30
	Irvine to Campbeltown	103 tons House Coal	Left November 7 Arr. November 7
	Campbeltown to Irvine	Ballast	Left December 6 Arr. December 6
	Irvine to Campbeltown	102 tons House Coal	Left December 15 Arr. December 15
	Campbeltown to Irvine	Ballast	Left December 22 Arr. December 22
		Half Year	
1922	Irvine to Campbeltown	100 tons House Coal	Left January 5 Arr. January 5
	Campbeltown to Irvine	Ballast	Left February 1 Arr. February 1
	Irvine to Campbeltown	102 tons House Coal	Left February 9 Arr. February 9
	Campbeltown to Irvine	Ballast	Left February 23 Arr. February 23
	Irvine to Campbeltown	104 tons House Coal	Left March 2 Arr. March 2
	Campbeltown to Irvine	Ballast	Left March 10 Arr. March 10
	Irvine to Campbeltown	100 tons House Coal	Left March 11 Arr. March 12
	Campbeltown to Irvine	Ballast	Left March 22 Arr. March 23
	Irvine to Campbeltown	103 tons House Coal	Left March 23 Arr. March 26
	Campbeltown to Irvine	Ballast	Left April 2 Arr. April 3
	Irvine to Campbeltown	103 tons House Coal	Left April 10 Arr. April 10
	Campbeltown to Irvine	Ballast	Left April 21 Arr.April 21
	Irvine to Campbeltown	104 tons House Coal	Left April 26 Arr. April 26
	Campbeltown to Irvine	Ballast	Left May 8 Arr. May 8
	Irvine to Campbeltown	103 tons House Coal	Left May 10 Arr. May 10
	Campbeltown to Irvine	Ballast	Left May 18 Arr. May 18
		Half Year	
	Irvine to Rostrevor	100 tons House Coal	Left August 31 Arr. September 2
	Rostrevor to Dublin	Ballast	Left September 8 Arr. September 9

	Dublin to Irvine	102 tons Scrap Iron	Left September 20 Arr. October 3
	Irvine to Dublin	100 tons Fire Clay	Left October 17 Arr. November 4
	Dublin to Irvine	108 tons Scrap Iron	Left November 25 Arr. December 2
		Half Year	
1923	Irvine to Dublin	100 tons Fire Clay	Left February 13 Arr. March 9
	Dublin to Irvine	105 tons Scrap Iron	Left April 3 Arr. April 13
	Irvine to Dublin	104 tons Fire Clay	Left May 22 Arr. May 24
	Dublin to Irvine	103 tons Scrap Iron	Left June 9 Arr. June 12
	Irvine to Wicklow	102 tons House Coal	Left July 18 Arr. July 26
	Wicklow to Dublin	Light	Left August 4 Arr. August 4
	Dublin to Connahs Quay	103 tons Light Scrap	Left August 13 Arr. August 15
	Connahs Quay to Dublin	101 tons Bricks & Tiles	Left August 27 Arr. September 13
	Dublin to Irvine	103 tons Scrap Iron	Left September 29 Arr. October 1
	Irvine to Dublin	101 tons Fire Clay Goods	Left October 18 Arr. November 2
	Dublin to Glasgow	103 tons Scrap Iron	Left December 10 Arr. December 13
1924	Glasgow to Kilkeel	102 tons Coal	Left January 2 Arr. January 13
	Kilkeel to Dublin	Ballast	Left March 31 Arr. April 1
	Dublin to Connahs Quay	103 tons Scrap Iron	Left April 8 Arr. April 19
	Connahs Quay to Dublin	95 tons Bricks & Tiles	Left May 5 Arr. May 19
	Dublin to Connahs Quay	98 tons Scrap Iron	Left June 2 Arr. June 16
	Connahs Quay to Annalong	100 tons Blue Bricks	Left June 20 Arr. July 1
	Annalong to Dublin	Ballast	Left July 21 Arr. July 22
	Dublin to Irvine	107 tons Scrap Iron	Left July 30 Arr. July 31
	Irvine to Troon	Light	Left August 20 Arr. August 20
	Troon to Wicklow	102 tons House Coal	Left August 23 Arr. August 24
	Wicklow to Dublin	Light	Left September 6 Arr. September 6
	Dublin to Glasgow	107 tons Scrap Iron	Left September 22 Arr. October 2
	Glasgow to Dublin	105 tons Molding Sand	Left November 1 Arr. November 7
1925	Dublin to Irvine 6/6	105 tons Scrap Iron	Left March 13 Arr. March 17
	Irvine to Dublin 10/-	106 tons Fireclay Pipes & Firebks.	Left March 25 Arr. March 28
	Dublin to Irvine 6/6	85 tons Scrap Iron	Left April 17 Arr. April 21
	Irvine to Dublin 10/-	105 tons Fireclay	Left Apr. 30 Arr. May 3
	Dublin to Irvine 6/6	104 tons Scrap Iron	Left May 19 Arr. May 22
	Irvine to Dublin 10/-	105 tons Pipes & Bricks	Left July 2 Arr. July 4

	Dublin to Glasgow 7/-	100 tons Scrap Iron	Left July 24 Arr. July 31
	Glasgow to Irvine	Ballast	Left August 7 Arr. August 10
	Irvine to Dublin 10/-	105 tons Pipes & Bricks	Left August 15 Arr. August 18
	Dublin to Connahs Quay 7/-	103 tons Scrap Iron	Left September 11 Arr. September 18
	Connahs Quay to Dublin 12/6	105 tons Fireclay Goods	Left October 2 Arr. ?
1926	Dublin to Irvine 6/6	103 tons Scrap Iron	Left March 29 Arr. April 10
	Irvine to Dublin 10/-	105 tons Fireclay Goods	Left April 13 Arr. April 20
	Dublin to Irvine	Ballast	Left May 6 Arr. May 22
	Irvine to Dublin 10/-	105 tons Fireclay	Left May 29 Arr. June 3
	Dublin to Glasgow 7/-	103 tons Scrap Iron	Left July 3 Arr. July 7
	Glasgow to Irvine	Ballast	Left July 17 Arr. July 20
	Irvine to Dublin 10/-	105 tons Fireclay	Left July 30 Arr. August 2
	Dublin to Glasgow 7/-	100 tons Scrap Iron	?
	Glasgow to Portavogie 7/-	100 tons House Coal	Left December 9 Arr. December 27
1927	Millbay of Plymouth Reg. 44 Tons		
	Portavogie to Irvine	Ballast	Left February 2 Arr. February 6
	Irvine to Castletown IOM 7/6	100 tons Coal & Fireclay	Left April 30 Arr. May 12
	Castletown to Connahs Quay	Ballast	Left May 18 Arr. May 19
	Connahs Quay to Belfast 7/6	100 tons Bricks & Tiles	Left May 30 Arr. June 1
	Belfast to Ayr	Ballast	Left July 4 Arr. July 5
	Ayr to Kilkeel	95 tons House Coal	Left July 10 Arr. July 10
	Kilkeel to Harrington	Ballast	Left July 22 Arr. July 23
	Harrington to Kilkeel	90 tons House Coal	Left July 26 Arr. July 28
	Kilkeel to Irvine	Ballast	Left August 3 Arr. August 4
	Irvine to Dublin	103 tons Fireclay Goods	Left August 10 Arr. August 15
	Dublin to Irvine	100 tons Scrap Iron	Left September 2 Arr. September 4
	Irvine to Portavogie	101 tons Bricks	Left September 12 Arr. September 13
	Portavogie to Irvine	Ballast	Left September 20 Arr. September 20
	Irvine to Portaferry	98 tons Bricks	Left September 24 Arr. September 27
	Portaferry to Irvine	Ballast	Left October 4 Arr. October 4

	Irvine to Skerries	105 tons House Coal	Left October 11 Arr. October 13
	Skerries to Irvine	Ballast	Left October 24 Arr. November 3
	Irvine to Dublin	100 tons Fireclay Goods	Left November 29 Arr. November 30
	Dublin to Irvine	102 tons Scrap Iron	Left December 13 Arr. January 18
1928	Irvine to Campbeltown	100 tons House Coal	Left February 3 Arr. February 3
	Campbeltown to Irvine	Ballast	Left February 19 Arr. February 19
	Irvine to Dublin	100 tons Fireclay Goods	Left February 25 Arr. February 27
	Dublin to Irvine	100 tons Scrap Iron	Left March 26 arr. March 27
	Irvine to Campbeltown	95 tons House Coal	Left April 6 Arr. April 6
	Campbeltown to Ayr	Light	Left April 19 Arr. April 19
	Ayr to Campbeltown	98 tons House Coal	Left April 21 Arr. April 21
	Campbeltown to Ayr	Light	Left May 1 Arr. May 1
	Ayr to Kilkeel	96 tons House Coal	Left May 4 Arr. May 5
	Kilkeel to Ayr	Light	Left May 15 Arr. May 23
	Ayr to Kilkeel	94 tons House Coal	Left May 25 Arr. May 28
	Kilkeel to Irvine	Light	Left June 12 arr. June 13
	Irvine to Dublin	100 tons Fireclay Goods	Left June 20 Arr. June 27
	Dublin to Irvine	101½ tons Scrap Iron	Left July 6 Arr. July 8
	Irvine to Ayr	Light	Left July 16 Arr. July 16
	Ayr to Kilkeel	95 tons House Coal	Left July 17 Arr. July 18
	Kilkeel to Irvine	Light	Left July 25 Arr. July 26
	Irvine to Teelin	100 tons House Coal	Left July 31 Arr. August 2
	Teelin to Donegal	Light	Left August 21 Arr. August 21
	Donegal to Campbeltown	75 tons Pailing Stabs	Left August 29 Arr. September 12
	Campbeltown to Irvine	Light	Left September 15 Arr. September 15
	Irvine to Dublin	100 tons Fireclay Goods	Left September 21 Arr. September 22
	Dublin to Campbeltown	77 tons Barley	Left November 5 Arr. November 7
	Campbeltown to Ayr	Light	Left November 28 Arr. November 28
	Ayr to Campbeltown	92 tons House Coal	Left December 3 Arr. December 4
	Campbeltown to Ayr	Light	Left December 17 Arr. December 17
	Ayr to Campbeltown	93 tons House Coal	Left December 27 Arr. December 28
		Half Year	

1929	Campbeltown to Ayr	Light	Left January 1 Arr. January 1
	Ayr to Campbeltown	93 tons House Coal	Left January 8 Arr. January 8
	Campbeltown to Ayr	Light	Left January 17 Arr. January 17
	Ayr to Campbeltown	96 tons House Coal	Left January 22 Arr. January 22
	Campbeltown to Ayr	Light	Left February 9 Arr. February 9
	Ayr to Campbeltown	97 tons House Coal	Left February 15 Arr. February 15
	Campbeltown to Ayr	Light	Left March 2 Arr. March 2
	Ayr to Campbeltown	95 tons House Coal	Left March 7 Arr. March 7
	Campbeltown to Ayr	Light	Left March 12 Arr. March 12
	Ayr to Campbeltown	99 tons House Coal	Left March 19 Arr. March 19
	Campbeltown to Ayr	Light	Left March 27 Arr. March 27
	Ayr to Kilkeel	96 tons House Coal	Left March 29 Arr. March 31
	Kilkeel to Irvine	Light	Left April 18 Arr. April 19
	Irvine to Teelin	98 tons House Coal	Left April 30 Arr. May 2
	Teelin to Irvine	Light	Left May 20 Arr. May 24
	Irvine to Teelin	98 tons House Coal	Left May 27 Arr. May 29
	Teelin to Donegal	Light	Left June 17 Arr. June 17
	Donegal to Campbeltown	73.6 tons Pailing Stabs	Left June 27 Arr. July 3
	Campbeltown to Irvine	Light	Left July 27 Arr. July 8
	Irvine to Teelin	100 tons House Coal	Left July 13 Arr. July 15
	Teelin to Donegal	Part Cargo	Left July 22 Arr. July 22
	Donegal to Irvine	Ballast	Left July 26 Arr. August 3
	Irvine to Killybegs	100 tons House Coal	Left August 26 Arr. August 28
	Killybegs to Irvine	Ballast	Left September 16 Arr. September 17
	Irvine to Ballydoran	100 tons House Coal	Left October 2 Arr. November 6
	Ballydoran to Belfast	Ballast	Left December 1 Arr. December 16
1930	Belfast to Irvine	102 tons Steel Scrap	Left January 15 Arr. January 16
	Irvine to Ballydoran	95 tons House Coal	Left February 2 Arr. February 8
	Ballydoran to Irvine	Ballast	Left March 24 Arr. March 27
	Irvine to Teelin	96 tons House Coal	Left April 11 Arr. April 22
	Teelin to Belfast	Ballast	Left May 15 Arr. May 16
	Belfast to Irvine	Ballast	Left May 21 Arr. May 22
	Irvine to Teelin	98 tons House Coal	Left May 24 Arr. May 31
	Teelin to Mullinasole	Ballast	Left June 12 Arr. June 12

	Mullinasole to Campbeltown	70 tons Pailing Posts	Left June 14 Arr. June 18
	Campbeltown to Irvine	Ballast	Left June 25 Arr. June 25
	Irvine to Donegal	95 tons House Coal	Left July 2 Arr. July 8
	Donegal to Mullaghmore	Light	Left July 13 Arr. July 13
	Mullaghmore to Bowling	95 tons Kelp	Left July 16 Arr. July 30
	Bowling to Irvine	Ballast	Left August 4 Arr. August 5
	Irvine to Donegal	98 tons House Coal	Left August 16 Arr. August 29
	Donegal to Burtonport	-	Left September 17
		Laid Up	October 29 1930
1931	Burtonport to Campbeltown	80 tons Pailing Stabs	Left March 27 Arr. April 9
	Campbeltown to Irvine	Light	Left April 21 Arr. April 21
	Irvine to Teelin	99 tons House Coal	Left May 2 Arr. May 7
	Teelin to Irvine	Ballast	Left May 26 Arr. May 28
	Irvine to Teelin	97 tons House Coal	Left June 8 Arr. June 10
	Teelin to Belfast	Ballast	Left June 30 Arr. July 1
	Belfast to Irvine	Ballast	Left July 4 Arr. July 4
		End of Half Year	
	Irvine to Donegal	99 tons House Coal	Left July 7 Arr. July 13
	Donegal to Irvine	98½ tons House Coal	Left August 1 Arr. August 3
	Donegal to Campbeltown	73 tons Pailing Stabs	Left August 24 Arr. August 29
	Campbeltown to Irvine	Ballast	Left August 31 Arr. August 31
	Irvine to Donegal	99 tons House Coal	Left September 5 Arr. September 9
1932	Laid up Since September		
	Donegal to Troon	50 tons Timber	Left April 25 Arr. May 17
	Troon to Irvine	Light	Left May 19 Arr. May 19
	Irvine to Teelin	98 tons House Coal	Left May 25 Arr. June 1
	Teelin to Irvine	Light	Left June 14 Arr. June 18
	Irvine to Donegal	99 tons House Coal	Left June 25 Arr. July 13
	Donegal to Teelin	Light	Left July 18 Arr. July 18
	Teelin to Sligo	Light	Left September 20 Arr. September 20
	Sligo to Teelin	Light	Left September 23 Arr. September 23
1933	Laid Up		
	Teelin to Killybegs	Light	Left April 1 Arr. April 1
	Killybegs to Belmullet	70 tons Oats	Left April 6 Arr. April 8

	Belmullet to Irvine	Light	Left April 12 Arr. April 24
	Irvine to Teelin	100 tons House Coal	Left April 29 Arr. May 4
	Teelin to Belfast	Light	Left May 20 Arr. May 22
	Belfast to Irvine	Light	Left May 25 Arr. May 25
	Irvine to Donegal	100 tons House Coal	Left May 29 Arr. June 5
	Donegal to Irvine	Light	Left June 14 Arr. July 1
	Irvine to Bruckless	94 tons House Coal	Left August 11 Arr. August 21
	Bruckless to Irvine	Light	Left August 29 Arr. August 30
	Irvine to Donegal	100 tons House Coal	Left September 5 Arr. September 7
	Donegal to Teelin	Light	Left September 18 Arr. September 18
	Laid Up		
1934	Teelin to Letterkenny	Light	Left March 24 Arr. March 26
	Letterkenny to Belmullet	70 tons Oats	Left March 30 Arr. April 1
	Belmullet to Irvine	Light	Left April 3 Arr. May 2
	Irvine to Teelin	100 tons House Coal	Left May 4 Arr. May 23
	Teelin to Irvine	Light	Left June 13 Arr. June 18
	Irvine to Douglas	100 tons Bricks	Left June 23 Arr. June 25
	Douglas to Irvine	Light	Left June 28 Arr. July 3
	Irvine to Donegal	100 tons House Coal	Left July 5 Arr. July 10
	Donegal to Downings	30 tons Part Cargo of Coal	Left July 14 Arr. July 18
	Downings to Irvine	Light	Left July 22 Arr. July 23
	Irvine to Donegal	95 tons 10 cwt. House Coal Inspected J.McHugh (Teelin 8/8/34)	Left August 1 Arr. August 10
	Donegal to Irvine	Light	Left August 18 Arr. August 29
	Irvine to Dublin	Fireclay Goods	Left September 5 Arr. September 15
	Dublin to Irvine	Light	Left October 15 Arr. October 25
	Irvine to Ringhaddy	100 tons House Coal	Left October 31 Arr. November 8
	Remained at Ringhaddy until Jan 16th/35		
1935	Ringhaddy to Irvine	Ballast	Left January 16 11am Arr.Feb.4 2pm
	Irvine to Dublin	98 tons Fireclay Goods	Left March 8 3pm Arr. Mar. 29 4pm
	Dublin to Irvine	Ballast	Left April 16 10pm Arr. April 22 1pm

	Irvine to Bruckless	100 tons House Coal	Left April 23 11pm Arr. April 30 4am
	Bruckless to Irvine	Ballast	Left May 3 5pm Arr. May 8 10pm
	Irvine to Wicklow	98 tons House Coal	Left May 20 10pm Arr. May 22 3pm
	Wicklow to Irvine	Ballast	Left May 28 11pm Arr.June 1 11am
	Irvine to Dublin	97 tons Fireclay Goods Inspected at Skerries P.J. Boyd HM 20/6/35	Left June 15 8am Arr. June 20 4pm
	Dublin to Preston	Ballast	Left June 29 9am Arr.July 2 2pm
	Preston to Donegal	96 tons House Coal	Left 7 July 2pm Arr.July 15 4pm
	Donegal to Irvine	Ballast	Left July 18 7am Arr. July 26 6pm
	Irvine to Troon	Ballast	Left August 13 11am Arr. Aug.13 1pm
	Troon to Port St. Mary	100 tons Bricks	Left August 14 6pm Arr. Aug. 16 2pm
	Port St. Mary to Whitehaven	Ballast	Left September 5 5am Arr. Sep.5 6pm
	Whitehaven to Balbriggan	95 tons House Coal	Left September 7 6am Arr. Oct. 9 10pm
	Balbriggan to Ayr	Ballast	Left October 15 2pm Arr. Oct. 24 7pm
	Ayr to Campbeltown	92 tons House Coal Inspected AJ Thomson HM Custom House Campbeltown 5/11/1935	Left November 1 11am Arr. Nov. 4 3pm
1936	Campbeltown to Troon	Ballast	Left November 8 8 am Arr. Nov. 8 4pm
	Troon to Campbeltown	90 tons House Coal	Left November 20 10am Arr. Nov. 20 5pm
	Campbeltown to Ayr	Ballast	Left November 24 7am Arr. Nov. 24 3pm
	Ayr to Campbeltown	95 tons House Coal	Left December 5 8am Arr. Dec. 5 5pm
	Campbeltown to Irvine	Ballast	Left December 12 9am Arr. Dec. 12 9pm
	Irvine to Campbeltown	96 tons House Coal Inspected Campbeltown AJ Thomson 9/1/36	Left January 8 8am Arr. Jan. 8 6pm
	Campbeltown to Ayr	Ballast	Left January 13 6am Arr. Jan. 13 3pm
	Ayr to Campbeltown	95 tons House Coal	Left January 16 9am Arr. Jan. 16 4pm

Campbeltown to Irvine	Ballast	Left January 22 7am Arr. Jan. 22 2pm
Irvine to Dublin	85 tons Fireclay Goods	Left January 29 2pm Arr. February 21 3pm
Dublin to Ardrossan	100 tons Scrap Iron	Left March 5 6am Arr. Mar. 12 5am
Ardrossan to Ayr	Ballast	Left March 21 10am Arr. Mar.21 2pm
Ayr to Campbeltown	97 tons House Coal	Left March 24 11am Arr. Mar.24 6pm
Campbeltown to Ayr	Ballast	Left March 31 8am Arr. Mar.31 3pm
Ayr to Campbeltown	98 tons House Coal	Left April 4 9am Arr. Apr.4 5pm
Campbeltown to Troon	Ballast	Left April 8 7am Arr. Apr.8 2pm
Troon to Campbeltown	95 tons House Coal	Left April 9 10am Arr. Apr.9 6pm
Campbeltown to Ayr	Ballast	Left April 14 8am Arr. Apr. 14 3pm
Ayr to Campbeltown	101 tons House Coal	Left April 16 11am Arr. Apr. 16 5pm
Campbeltown to Irvine	Ballast	Left April 20 7am Arr. Apr. 20 2pm
Irvine to Bruckless	99 tons House Coal	Left Apr. 21 3pm Arr. May 2 4pm
Bruckless to Irvine	Ballast Inspected Irvine 14/5/36 Custom House Irvine	Left May 7 5pm Arr. May 13 9am
Irvine to Donegal	98 tons House Coal	Left May 16 4pm Arr. May 23 5pm
Donegal to Dublin	Ballast	Left May 27 10am Arr. June 13 11am
Dublin to Teelin	60 tons Timber	Left June 19 4am Arr. June 22 8pm
Teelin to Londonderry	Ballast	Left July 1 4pm Arr. July 2 5am
Londonderry to Glasgow	100 tons Scrap Iron	Left July 4 2pm Arr. July 5 11pm
Glasgow to Donegal	95 tons House Coal	Left July 12 8am Arr. July 18 4pm
Donegal to Irvine	Ballast	Left July 26 5am Arr. August 10 6pm
Irvine to Belmullet	100 tons House Coal	Left August 18 8am Arr. Sep. 2 4pm
Belmullet to Irvine	43 tons Scrap Iron	Left September 18 6am Arr. Sep. 20 11pm
Irvine to Ringhaddy	98 tons House Coal	Left September 23 6pm Arr. Sep.26 4pm
Ringhaddy to Irvine	Ballast	Left October 28 9am Arr. Oct.31 11pm

	Irvine to Ringniel	98 tons House Coal	Left November 18 9am Arr. Nov. 19 11am
1937	Ringhaddy to Troon	24 tons Potatoes	Left January 25 am Arr. Feb. 5 pm
	Troon to Ballydoran	100 tons Brick	Left February 23 pm Arr. Mar.15 pm
	Ballydoran to Irvine	Ballast	Left April 19 am Arr. Apr.21 pm
	Irvine to Bruckless	100 tons House Coal	Left May 6 pm Arr. May 10 am
	Bruckless to Mulroy Bay	Ballast	Left May 17 pm Arr. May 18 am
	Mulroy Bay to Irvine	71 tons Scrap Iron	Left May 30 am Arr. May 31 am
	Irvine to Londonderry	100 tons House Coal	Left June 10 pm Arr. June 11 pm
	Londonderry to Glasgow	100 tons Scrap	Left June 17 pm Arr. June 20 pm
	Glasgow to Irvine	Ballast Inspected Irvine 2 Jul 1937	Left June 30 am Arr. July 1 pm
	Irvine to Donegal	98 tons House Coal	Left July 17 am Arr. July 22 pm
	Donegal to Londonderry	Ballast	Left July 28 pm Arr. July 29 am
	Londonderry to Irvine	100 tons Scrap Iron	Left July 29 pm Arr. July 31 pm
	Irvine to Londonderry	100 tons House Coal	Left August 3 am Arr. Aug. 4 am
	Londonderry to Irvine	100 tons Scrap Iron	Left August 13 pm Arr. Aug.14 pm
	Irvine to Donegal	100 tons House Coal 1937 Sep.6 Inspected Donegal	Left August 26 am Arr. Sept. 4 pm
	Donegal to Bunbeg	In Ballast	Left Sept. 27 pm Arr. Sep.28 pm
	Bunbeg to Irvine	75 tons Scrap Iron	Left October 2 pm Arr. Oct. 4 pm
	Irvine to Ringhaddy	96 tons House Coal	Left October 20 am Arr. Oct. 22 pm
	Ringhaddy to Troon	Ballast	Left December 1 am Arr. Dec.23 pm
	Troon to Campbeltown	97 ? (cargo omitted in log) Inspected AJT Thomson 30/12/37.P.o/C Campbeltown	Left December 29 Arr. Dec. 29 pm
1938	Campbeltown to Troon	Ballast 5/1/38 Troon Inspected G. Stewart PO H.M. Customs Troon	Left January 1 Arr. Jan. 1 pm
	Troon to Campbeltown	98 tons House Coal	Left February 6 am Arr. Feb. 6 pm
	Campbeltown to Troon	Ballast	Left February 15 pm Arr. Feb. 15 pm

Troon to Campbeltown	97 tons House Coal	Left February 17 pm Arr. Feb. 17 pm
Campbeltown to Troon	Ballast	Left February 24 am Arr. Feb.24 pm
Troon to Campbeltown	97 tons House Coal	Left February 27 am Arr. Mar. 4 pm
Campbeltown to Troon	Ballast	Left March 18 Arr. March 18
Troon to Campbeltown	98 tons House Coal	Left March 23 Arr. March26
Campbeltown to Troon	Ballast	Left April 1 Arr. April 1
Troon to Campbeltown	100 tons House Coal	Left April 9 Arr. April 9
Campbeltown to Troon	Ballast	Left April 19 Arr. April 19
Troon to Campbeltown	102 tons House Coal	Left April 21 Arr. April 21
Campbeltown to Troon	Ballast	Left May 4 Arr. May 4
Troon to Campbeltown	100 tons Coal	Left May 6 Arr. May 6
Campbeltown to Troon	Ballast	Left May 10 Arr. May 10
Troon to Campbeltown	97 tons House Coal	Left May 12 Arr. May 12
Campbeltown to Irvine	Ballast	Left May 19 Arr. May 19
Irvine to Bruckless	100 tons House Coal	Left May 28 Arr. June 14
Bruckless to Londonderry	Ballast Inspected 3/7/38 Londonderry	Left June 30 Arr. July 2
	Half Year	
Londonderry to Ardrossan	95 tons Scrap Iron	Left July 4 Arr. July 5
Ardrossan to Ayr	Ballast	Left July 7 Arr. July 7
Ayr to Coleraine	93 tons House Coal	Left July 8 Arr. July 13
Coleraine to Irvine	70 tons Scrap Iron Inspected Irvine 26/7/38	Left July 22 Arr. July 26
1938 July 28 Inspd.RN off Ayr		
Irvine to Londonderry	99 tons House Coal	Left August 3 Arr. Aug. 4
Londonderry to Ardrossan	98 tons Scrap Iron	Left August 11 Arr. Aug. 13
Ardrossan to Irvine	Ballast	Left August 21 Arr. Aug. 21
Irvine to Teelin	97 tons House Coal	Left August 31 Arr. Sep. 2
Teelin to Donegal	Ballast	Left September 20 Arr. Sep. 21
Donegal to Londonderry	50 tons Part Cargo Scrap Iron	Left September 29 Arr. Sep. 30
Londonderry to Ardrossan	50 tons Scrap Iron	Left October 7 Arr. Oct. 20
Ardrossan to Irvine	Ballast	Left October 22 Arr. Oct. 22
Irvine to Ringhaddy	98 tons House Coal	Left october 27 Arr. Oct. 28

	Laid Up 26/11/38 at Ringhaddy		
1939	Inspected 9 January 1939		
	Ringhaddy to Troon	Ballast	Left February 24 Arr. Mar. 9
	Troon to Teelin	95 tons House Coal	Left April 1 Arr. Apr. 6
	Teelin to Irvine	Ballast Inspected R.Mele PO Irvine 6 May 1939	Left April 26 Arr. May 6
	Irvine to Bruckless	96 tons House Coal	Left May 11 Arr. May 15
	Bruckless to Killybegs	Ballast	Left May 23 Arr. May 23
	Killybegs to Irvine	82 tons Scrap Iron	Left June 1 Arr. June 5
	Irvine to Donegal	99 tons House Coal	Left June 7 Arr. June 28
	Donegal to Ballina	Ballast	Left July 3 am Arr. July 5 pm
	Ballina to Campbeltown	40 tons Dried Seaweed	Left July 6 pm Arr. July 8 am
	Campbeltown to Troon	Ballast	Left July 11 am Arr. July 11 pm
	Troon to Campbeltown	98 tons House Coal	Left July 14 am Arr. July 14 pm
	Campbeltown to Irvine	Ballast	Left July 20 am Arr. July 20 pm
	Irvine to Killybegs	100 tons House Coal	Left July 24 pm Arr. Aug. 4 pm
	Killybegs to Irvine	Ballast	Left August 28 am Arr. Sep. 2
	Irvine to Rothesay	90 tons Bricks Inspected Rothesay 16/9/39	Left September 15 am Arr. Sep. 15 pm
	Rothesay to Irvine	Ballast	Left September 17 Arr. Sep. 17 am
	Irvine to Campbeltown	101 tons House Coal Inspected Campbeltown AJT Thomson 27/9/39	Left September 26 am Arr. Sep.26 pm
	Campbeltown to Irvine	Ballast	Left September 28 Arr. Sep. 30 pm
	Irvine to Campbeltown	98 tons Bricks	Left September 30 am Arr. Sep. 30 pm
	Campbeltown to Irvine	Ballast	Left October 7 am Arr. Oct. 7 pm
	Irvine to Campbeltown	98 tons House Coal Inspected Irvine 10/10/39	Left October 10 pm Arr. Oct. 11 am
	Campbeltown to Irvine	Ballast	Left October 14 am Arr. Oct. 15 am
	Irvine to Campbeltown	93 tons House Coal	Left October 16 pm Arr. Oct. 17 am
	Campbeltown to Irvine	Ballast	Left October 18 am Arr. Oct. 19 am
	Irvine to Campbeltown	99 tons House Coal	Left October 19 pm Arr. Oct. 20 am

	Campbeltown to Irvine	Ballast	Left October 21 am Arr. Oct. 21 pm
	Irvine to Campbeltown	97 tons House Coal	Left October 24 am Arr. Oct. 24 pm
	Campbeltown to Troon	Ballast	Left October 27 am Arr. Oct. 27 pm
	Troon to Campbeltown	99 tons House Coal	Left October 30 am Arr. Oct. 30 pm
	Campbeltown to Irvine	Ballast	Left November 5 am Arr. Nov. 5 pm
	Irvine to Campbeltown	71 tons Coal & Tiles	Left November 17 Arr. Nov. 20 pm
	Campbeltown to Irvine	Ballast	Left November 30 am Arr. Nov. 30 pm
	Irvine to Campbeltown	90 tons House Coal & Wood	Left December 8 Arr. Dec. 9
	Campbeltown to Irvine	Ballast	Left December 18 am Arr. Dec. 19 am
	Irvine to Campbeltown	95 tons House Coal & Tiles	Left December 22 pm Arr. Dec. 23 am
	Campbeltown to Irvine	Ballast	Left December 26 Arr. Dec. 26 pm
	Irvine to Campbeltown	100 tons House Coal	Left December 28 pm Arr. Dec. 29 am
	Campbeltown to Irvine Inspected AJT Thomson Custom House Campbeltown 23.Jan.1940	Ballast	Left December 30 pm Arr. Dec. 31 am
1940	Irvine to Campbeltown	82 tons House Coal	Left January 21 am Arr. Jan 21 pm
	Campbeltown to Troon	Ballast	Left February 8 am Arr. Feb. 8 pm
	Troon to Irvine	Ballast	Left February 15 pm Arr. Feb. 15 pm
	Irvine to Campbeltown	91 tons House Coal	Left February 22 am Arr. Feb. 22 pm
	Campbeltown to Irvine Inspected Irvine 5 Mar.1940	Ballast	Left March 2 am Arr. Mar. 2 pm
	Irvine to Campbeltown	91 tons House Coal	Left March 5 pm Arr. March 6 am
	Campbeltown to Irvine	Ballast	Left March 7 am Arr. Mar. 7 pm
	Irvine to Campbeltown	90 tons House Coal & Tiles	Left March 13 am Arr. Mar. 13 pm
	Campbeltown to Irvine	Ballast	Left March 16 am Arr. Mar. 16 pm
	Irvine to Campbeltown	102 tons House Coal	Left March 22 am Arr. Mar. 22 pm

Campbeltown to Irvine	Ballast	Left March 25 am Arr. Mar. 25 pm
Irvine to Campbeltown Exd. Cargo Inspected AJT Thomson Custom House Campbeltown 28 Mar. 1940	99 tons House Coal	Left March 27 am Arr. Mar. 27 pm
Campbeltown to Irvine	Ballast	Left March 30 am Arr. Mar. 30 pm
Irvine to Campbeltown	90 tons House Coal	Left April 2 pm Arr. Apr. 5 pm
Campbeltown to Irvine	Ballast	Left April 8 am Arr. Apri. 8 pm
Irvine to Campbeltown	100 tons House Coal & Tiles	Left April 11 pm Arr. Apr. 12 am
Campbeltown to Irvine	Ballast	Left April 16 am Arr. Apr. 16 pm
Irvine to Campbeltown	98 tons House Coal	Left April 18 pm Arr. Apr. 19 am
Campbeltown to Irvine	Ballast	Left April 24 am Arr. Apr. 24 pm
Irvine to Campbeltown	92 tons House Coal	Left May 2 am Arr. May 3 am
Campbeltown to Carrickfergus Inspected C'fergus 20/5/40	Ballast Getting Engine Repaired	Left May 18 am Arr. May 20 am
Carrickfergus to Carnlough Inspected at Carnlough 1/9/40	Ballast	Left August 31 Arr. Aug. 31
Carnlough to Irvine	100 tons Limestone	Left September 4 Arr. Sep. 6
Irvine to Campbeltown	93 tons House Coal	Left September 11 Arr. Sep. 11
Campbeltown to Irvine	Ballast	Left September 14 Arr. Sep. 14
Irvine to Campbeltown	101 tons House Coal	Left September 21 Arr. Sep. 24
Campbeltown to Irvine	Ballast	Left October 1 Arr. Oct. 2
Irvine to Campbeltown	104 tons House Coal	Left October 3 Arr. Oct. 4
Campbeltown to Irvine	Ballast	Left October 10 Arr. Oct. 10
Irvine to Rothesay	82 tons Steam Coal	Left October 11 Arr. Oct. 12
Rothesay to Irvine	Ballast	Left October 24 Arr. Oct. 24
Irvine to Campbeltown	104 tons House Coal & Tiles	Left October 25 Arr. Oct. 26
Campbeltown to Irvine	Ballast	Left November 2 Arr. Nov. 2
Irvine to Campbeltown	96 tons House Coal	Left November 6 Arr. Nov. 6
Campbeltown to Irvine	Ballast	Left November 11 Arr. Nov. 11
Irvine to Campbeltown	93 tons House Coal	Left November 13 Arr. Nov. 14
Campbeltown to Irvine	Ballast	Left November 18 Arr. Nov. 18
Irvine to Campbeltown	98 tons House Coal	Left November 27 Arr. Nov. 27

	Campbeltown to Irvine	Ballast	Left December 4 Arr. Dec. 4
	Irvine to Campbeltown	95 tons House Coal & Tiles	Left December 12 Arr. Dec. 12
	Campbeltown to Irvine	Ballast	Left December 19 Arr. Dec. 20
	Irvine to Campbeltown	97 tons House Coal	Left December 20 Arr. Dec. 23
	Campbeltown to Irvine	Ballast	Left December 26 Arr. Dec. 27
	Irvine to Campbeltown	86 tons Coal, Tiles & Castings	Left December 30 Arr. Dec. 30
1941	Campbeltown to Irvine	Ballast	Left January 8 Arr. Jan. 9
	Irvine to Lamlash	100 tons Bricks	Left January 10 Arr. Jan. 10
	Lamlash to Irvine	Ballast	Left January 15 Arr. Jan. 15
	Irvine to Campbeltown	98 tons House Coal	Left January 23 Arr. Jan. 23
	Campbeltown to Irvine	Ballast	Left February 2 Arr. Feb. 2
	Irvine to Campbeltown	98 tons House Coal	Left February 6 Arr. Feb. 9
	Campbeltown to Irvine	Ballast	Left February 15 Arr. Feb. 15
	Irvine to Campbeltown	102 tons House Coal	Left February 19 Arr. Feb. 19
	Campbeltown to Irvine	Ballast	Left February 23 Arr. Feb. 23
	Irvine to Campbeltown	100 tons Bricks	Left February 25 Arr. Feb. 25
	Campbeltown to Irvine	Ballast	Left March 3 Arr. Mar.3
	Irvine to Campbeltown	100 tons Bricks	Left March 5 Arr. March 5
	Campbeltown to Troon	Ballast	Left March 11 Arr. Mar. 11
	Troon to Campbeltown	92 tons House Coal	Left March 13 Arr. Mar. 13
	Campbeltown to Troon	Ballast	Left March 16 Arr. Mar. 16
	Troon to Campbeltown	95 tons House Coal	Left March 18 Arr. Mar. 19
	Campbeltown to Irvine	Ballast	Left March 23 Arr. Mar. 23
	Irvine to Campbeltown	100 tons Bricks	Left March 25 Arr. Mar. 25
	Campbeltown to Troon	Ballast	Left March 30 Arr. Mar. 30
	Troon to Campbeltown	96 tons House Coal	Left April 5 Arr. Apr. 5
	Campbeltown to Troon	Ballast	Left Apr. 9 Arr. Apr. 10
	Troon to Campbeltown	95 tons House Coal	Left April 12 Arr. Apr. 12
	Campbeltown to Irvine	Ballast	Left April 16 Arr. Apr. 16
	Irvine to Rothesay	100 tons House Coal	Left April 18 Arr. Apr. 18
	Rothesay to Irvine	Ballast	Left April 24 Arr. Apr. 24
	Irvine to Tarbert	91 tons House Coal	Left April 26 Arr. April 26
	Tarbert to Irvine	Ballast	Left April 29 Arr. Apr. 29
	Irvine to Campbeltown	100 tons Bricks	Left May 2 Arr. May 2
	Campbeltown to Irvine	Ballast	Left May 6 Arr. May 7

Irvine to Campbeltown	96 tons House Coal	Left May 8 Arr. May 8
Campbeltown to Troon	Ballast	Left May 13 Arr. May 13
Troon to Campbeltown	95 tons House Coal	Left May 15 Arr. May 15
Campbeltown to Irvine	Ballast	Left May 29 Arr. May 29
Irvine to Rothesay	100 tons House Coal	Left May 30 Arr. May 30
Rothesay to Irvine	Ballast	Left June 7 Arr. June 8
Irvine to Rothesay	100 tons House Coal	Left June 9 Arr. June 9
Rothesay to Irvine	Ballast	Left June 13 Arr. June 13
Irvine to Campbeltown	101 tons Bricks	Left June 16 Arr. June 16
Campbeltown to Irvine	Ballast	Left June 17 Arr. June 17
Irvine to Loch Strivin	100 Cases Ammonal 3 Cases Detonators 660 Cases Gelignite	Left June 20 Arr. June 20
Loch Strivin to Belfast	3 Cases Detonators 6 Cases Electric Detonators 100 Cases Ammonal	Left June 21 Arr. June 24
Belfast to Carrickfergus	Ballast	Left June 26 Arr. June 26
Carrickfergus to Carnlough Inspected at Carnlough 18/7/41 D.F. Bowles	Ballast	Left July 18 Arr. July 18
Carnlough to Irvine	100 tons Limestone	Left July 20 Arr. July 20
Irvine to Campbeltown	100 tons Brick	Left July 22 Arr. July 22
Campbeltown to Irvine	Ballast	Left July 25 Arr. July 25
Irvine to Inveraray	100 tons House Coal	Left July 28 Arr. July 29
Inveraray to Irvine	Ballast	Left August 1 Arr. Aug. 2
Irvine to Crarae	Ballast	Left August 8 Arr. Aug. 8
Crarae to Campbeltown	100 tons Granite Chips	Left August 5 Arr. Aug. 5
Campbeltown to Troon	Ballast	Left August 8 Arr. Aug. 8
Troon to Tarbert	100 tons House Coal	Left August 14 Arr. Aug. 14
Tarbert to Irvine	Ballast	Left August 16 Arr. Aug. 16
Irvine to Inveraray	97 tons House Coal	Left August 20 Arr. Aug. 20
Inveraray to Irvine	Ballast	Left August 22 Arr. Aug. 23
Irvine to Inveraray	99 tons House Coal	Left August 28 Arr. Aug. 29
Inveraray to Irvine	Ballast	Left September 2 Arr. Sep. 2
Irvine to Inveraray	100 tons House Coal	Left September 3 Arr. Sep. 4
Inveraray to Irvine	Ballast	Left September 5 Arr. Sep. 6
Irvine to Inveraray	99 tons House Coal	Left September 6 Arr. Sep. 7
Inveraray to Irvine	Ballast	Left September 9 Arr. Sep. 10

	Irvine to Ardrishaig Inspected at Ardrishaig 14/9/41	97 tons House Coal	Left September 12 Arr. Sep. 12
	Ardrishaig to Irvine	Ballast	Left September 16 Arr. Sep. 16
	Irvine to Rothesay	99 tons Bricks	Left September 17 Arr. Sep. 17
	Rothesay to Irvine	Ballast	Left September 19 Arr. Sep. 19
	Irvine to Inveraray	100 tons House Coal & Coke	Left September 22 Arr. Sep. 23
	Inveraray to Irvine	Ballast	Left September 25 Arr. Sep. 29
	Irvine to Rothesay	85 tons House Coal	Left October 2 Arr. Oct. 2
	Rothesay to Irvine	Ballast	Left October 4 Arr. Oct. 4
	Irvine to Inveraray	99 tons House Coal	Left October 7 Arr. Oct. 8
	Inveraray to Irvine	Ballast	Left October 10 Arr. Oct. 12
	Irvine to Inveraray	101 tons House Coal	Left October 22 Arr. Oct. 23
	Inveraray to Irvine	Ballast	Left October 24 Arr. Oct. 25
	Irvine to Rothesay	94 tons House Coal	Left October 25 Arr. Oct. 26
	Rothesay to Irvine	Ballast	Left October 30 Arr. Oct. 30
	Irvine to Inveraray	100 tons House Coal	Left October 31 Arr. Nov. 3
	Inveraray to Irvine	Ballast	Left November 4 Arr. Nov. 5
	Irvine to Inveraray	100 tons House Coal	Left November 5 Arr. Nov. 7
	Inveraray to Irvine	Ballast	Left November 12 Arr. Nov. 13
	Irvine to Inveraray	98 tons House Coal	Left November 14 Arr. Nov. 17
	Inveraray to Irvine	Ballast	Left November 19 Arr. Nov. 28
	Irvine to Inveraray	90 tons House Coal	Left November 30 Arr. Dec. 1
	Inveraray to Irvine	Ballast	Left December 3 Arr. Dec. 4
	Irvine to Inveraray	100 tons House Coal	Left December 18 Arr. December 19
	Inveraray to Irvine	Ballast	Left December 23 Arr. Dec. 25
	Irvine to Inveraray	99 tons House Coal	Left December 27 Arr. Dec. 28
1942	Inveraray to Irvine	Ballast	Left December 30 Arr. Dec. 31
	Irvine to Inveraray	100 tons House Coal	Left January 6 Arr. Jan. 7
	Inveraray to Irvine	Ballast	Left January 8 Arr. Jan. 9
	Irvine to Troon	Ballast	Left January 9 Arr. Jan. 9
	Troon to Lamlash	96 tons House Coal	Left January 11 Arr. Jan. 11
	Lamlash to Irvine	Ballast	Left January 14 Arr. Jan. 14
	Irvine to Inveraray	97 tons House Coal	Left January 15 Arr. Jan. 18
	Inveraray to Irvine	Ballast	Left January 20 Arr. Jan. 28

Irvine to Inveraray	97 tons House Coal	Left January 31 Arr. Feb. 1
Inveraray to Irvine	Ballast	Left February 3 Arr. Feb. 5
Irvine to Inveraray	98 tons House Coal	Left February 7 Arr. Feb. 8
Inveraray to Irvine	Ballast	Left February 13 Arr. Feb. 13
Irvine to Inveraray	98 tons House Coal	Left February 14 Arr. Feb. 15
Inveraray to Irvine	Ballast	Left February 17 Arr. Feb. 17
Irvine to Inveraray	100 tons House Coal	Left February 19 Arr Feb. 20
Inveraray to Irvine	Ballast	Left February 21 Arr. Feb. 22
Irvine to Inveraray	100 tons House Coal	Left February 24 Arr. Feb. 25
Inveraray to Irvine	Ballast	Left February 28 Arr. Mar. 9
Irvine to Kilchattin Bay	100 tons Ground Lime	Left March 10 Arr. March 11
Kilchattin Bay to Irvine	Ballast	Left March 13 Arr. Mar. 13
Irvine to Inveraray	98 tons House Coal	Left March 15 Arr. Mar. 16
Inveraray to Irvine	Ballast	Left March 17 Arr. Mar. 18
Irvine to Inveraray	99 tons House Coal	Left March 19 Arr. Mar. 20
Inveraray to Irvine	Ballast	Left March 21 Arr. Mar. 22
Irvine to Inveraray	96 tons House Coal	Left March 23 Arr. Mar. 25
Inveraray to Irvine	Ballast	Left March 26 Arr. Mar. 27
Irvine to Inveraray	100 tons House Coal	Left March 28 Arr. Mar. 30
Inveraray to Irvine	Ballast	Left March 31 Arr. Apr. 2
Irvine to Campbeltown	100 tons House Coal	Left April 4 Arr. Apr. 7
Campbeltown to Irvine	Ballast	Left April 10 Arr. Apr. 10
Irvine to Inveraray	100 tons House Coal	Left April 14 Arr. Apr. 15
Inveraray to Troon	Ballast	Left April 16 Arr. Apr. 17
Troon to Rothesay	100 tons House Coal	Left April 18 Arr. Apr. 18
Rothesay to Ayr	Ballast	Left April 22 Arr. Apr. 22
Ayr to Tarbert	98 tons House Coal	Left April 23 Arr. Apr. 23
Tarbert to Irvine	Ballast	Left April 30 Arr. Apr. 30
Irvine to Inveraray	95 tons House Coal	Left May 2 Arr. May 3
Inveraray to Irvine	Ballast	Left May 4 Arr. May 5
Irvine to Inveraray	100 tons House Coal	Left May 7 Arr. May 12
Inveraray to Irvine	Ballast	Left May 13 Arr. May 14
Irvine to Inveraray	100 tons House Coal	Left May 14 Arr. May 15
Inveraray to Irvine	Ballast	Left May 18 Arr. May 18
Irvine to Inveraray	100 tons House Coal	Left May 20 Arr. May 20
Inveraray to Irvine	Ballast	Left May 21 Arr. May 22

	Irvine to Inveraray Inspected Inveraray 29/5/42	98 tons House Coal	Left May 28 Arr. May 28
	Inveraray to Irvine	Ballast	Left May 30 Arr. May 30
	Irvine to Inveraray	98 tons House Coal	Left June 3 Arr. June 3
	Inveraray to Irvine	Ballast	Left June 5 Arr. June 5
	Irvine to Inveraray	100 tons House Coal	Left June 10 Arr. June 10
	Inveraray to Irvine	Ballast	Left June 12 Arr. June 13
	Irvine to Inveraray	100 tons House Coal	Left June 16 Arr. June 16
	Inveraray to Irvine	Ballast	Left June 18 Arr. June 19
	Irvine to Inveraray	99 tons House Coal	Left June 20 Arr. June 21
	Inveraray to Irvine	Ballast	Left June 23 Arr. June 23
	Irvine to Inveraray	100 tons House Coal	Left June 27 Arr. June 28
	Inveraray to Irvine Inspected 7/7/42	Ballast	Left June 30 Arr. July 7
	Irvine to Inveraray	100 tons House Coal	Left July 7 Arr. July 7
	Inveraray to Irvine	Ballast	Left July 11 Arr. July 11
	Irvine to Inveraray	100 tons House Coal	Left July 13 Arr. July 14
	Inveraray to Irvine	Ballast	Left July 16 Arr. July 16
	Irvine to Inveraray	100 tons House Coal	Left July 18 Arr. July 20
	Inveraray to Irvine	Ballast	Left July 22 Arr. July 23
	Irvine to Inveraray	100 tons House Coal	Left July 30 Arr. July 31
	Inveraray to Ayr	Ballast	Left August 4 Arr. Aug. 5
	Ayr to Carnlough	91 tons House Coal	Left August 6 Arr. Aug. 9
	Carnlough to Carrickfergus	Ballast	Left August 13 Arr. Aug. 13
	Carrickfergus to Irvine	Ballast	Left September 17 Arr. Sep. 18
	Irvine to Campbeltown	627 Empty Milk Cans	Left September 24 Arr. Sep. 24
	Campbeltown to Irvine	30 tins Condensed Milk	Left September 26 Arr. Sep.26
	Irvine to Campbeltown	691 Empty Milk Cans	Left September 29 Arr. Sep. 29
	Campbeltown to Irvine	30 tons Condensed Milk	Left October 1 Arr. Oct. 2
	Irvine to Campbeltown	554 Empty Milk Cans	Left October 3 Arr. Oct. 4
	Campbeltown to Irvine	30 tons Condensed Milk	Left October 6 Arr. Oct. 6
	Irvine to Campbeltown	495 Empty Milk Cans	Left October 12 Arr. Oct. 13
	Campbeltown to Irvine	30 tons Condensed Milk	Left October 17 Arr. Oct. 17
	Irvine to Troon	Ballast	Left October 19 Arr. Oct. 19
	Troon to Whiting Bay Lamlash Inspected J.Ross PO 28/10/42	98 tons House Coal	Left October 27 Arr. Oct. 27

	Lamlash to Campbeltown	Ballast	Left October 27 Arr. Oct. 28
	Campbeltown to Irvine	29 tons Condensed Milk	Left October 30 Arr. Oct. 31
	Irvine to Brodick Pier	70 tons Bricks & Tiles	Left November 3 Arr. Nov. 3
	Brodick Pier to Campbeltown	Ballast	Left November 5 Arr. Nov. 5
	Campbeltown to Irvine	29 tons Condensed Milk	Left November 7 Arr. Nov. 7
	Irvine to Troon	Ballast	Left November 10 Arr. Nov. 10
	Troon to Whiting Bay	98 tons House Coal	Left November 11 Arr. Nov. 11
	Whiting Bay to Campbeltown	Ballast	Left November 13 Arr. Nov. 13
	Campbeltown to Irvine	29 tons Condensed Milk	Left November 15 Arr. Nov. 15
	Irvine to Whiting Bay	100 tons Lime	Left November 17 Arr. Nov. 17
	Whiting Bay to Irvine	Ballast	Left November 19 Arr. Nov. 19
	Irvine to Whiting Bay	88 tons Lime	Left November 24 Arr. Nov. 24
	Whiting Bay to Troon	Ballast	Left November 25 Arr. Nov. 25
	Troon to Whiting Bay	99 tons House Coal	Left November 27 Arr. Nov. 27
	Whiting Bay to Irvine	Ballast	Left December 2 Arr. Dec. 2
	Irvine to Lamlash	100 tons Lime	Left December 21 Arr. Dec. 21
	Lamlash to Irvine	Ballast	Left December 27 Arr. Dec. 27
1943	Irvine to Lamlash	100 tons General	Left January 3 Arr. Jan. 3
	Lamlash to Irvine	Ballast	Left January 10 Arr. Jan. 10
	Irvine to Campbeltown	98 tons Bricks	Left January 17 Arr. Jan. 17
	Campbeltown to Irvine	Ballast	Left January 21 Arr. Jan. 21
	Irvine to Campbeltown	99 tons House Coal	Left January 30 Arr. Jan. 31
	Campbeltown to Irvine	Ballast	Left February 2 Arr. Feb. 3
	Irvine to Lamlash	90 tons Limestone	Left February 9 Arr. Feb. 9
	Lamlash to Irvine	Ballast	Left February 13 Arr. Feb. 13
	Irvine to Campbeltown	75 tons Steam Coal	Left February 17 Arr. Feb. 18
	Campbeltown to Brodick	20 tons Limestone	Left February 20 Arr. Feb. 22
	Brodick to Irvine	Ballast	Left February 22 Arr. Feb. 22
	Irvine to Rothesay	85 tons Steam Coal	Left February 26 Arr. Feb. 27
	Rothesay to Irvine	Ballast	Left March 2 Arr. Mar. 2
	Irvine to Rothesay	100 tons Limestone	Left March 3 Arr. Mar. 3
	Rothesay to Irvine	Ballast	Left March 6 Arr. Mar. 6
	Irvine to Brodick	80 tons Limestone	Left March 7 Arr. Mar. 7
	Brodick to Irvine	Ballast	Left March 9 Arr. Mar. 9

Irvine to Campbeltown	100 tons Brick	Left March 12 Arr. Mar. 12
Campbeltown to Irvine	Ballast	Left March 17 Arr. Mar. 17
Irvine to Rothesay	99 tons Ground Lime	Left March 24 Arr. Mar. 24
Rothesay to Irvine	Ballast	Left March 27 Arr. Mar. 27
Irvine to Millport	100 tons Ground Limestone	Left April 2 Arr. Apr. 2
Millport to Irvine	Ballast	Left April 3 Arr. Apr. 3
Irvine to Rothesay	99 tons Ground Limestone	Left April 9 Arr. Apr. 10
Rothesay to Irvine	Ballast	Left April 13 Arr. Apr. 14
Irvine to Campbeltown	100 tons Bricks	Left April 15 Arr. Apr. 15
Campbeltown to Irvine	Ballast	Left April 17 Arr. Apr. 17
Irvine to Strachur	100 tons House Coal	Left April 21 Arr. Apr. 21
Strachur to Irvine	Ballast	Left April 24 Arr. Apr. 24
Irvine to Campbeltown	90 tons Coal & Tiles	Left April 28 Arr. Apr. 28
Campbeltown to Irvine	Ballast	Left May 1 Arr. May 1
Irvine to Rothesay	80 tons Bricks	Left May 3 Arr. May 3
Rothesay to Irvine	Ballast	Left May 5 Arr. May 5
Irvine to Inveraray	95 tons House Coal	Left May 6 Arr. May 7
Inveraray to Troon	Ballast	Left May 10 Arr. May 13
Troon to Rothesay	96 tons House Coal	Left May 14 Arr. May 15
Rothesay to Irvine	Ballast	Left May 18 Arr. May 18
Irvine to Campbeltown	95 tons Bricks	Left May 19 Arr. May 19
Campbeltown to Irvine	Ballast	Left May 21 Arr. May 21
Irvine to Rothesay	85 tons Bricks	Left May 22 Arr. May 22
Rothesay to Irvine	Ballast	Left May 25 Arr. May 26
Irvine to Strachur	85 tons House Coal	Left May 28 Arr. May 28
Strachur to Irvine	Ballast	Left May 29 Arr. May 30
Irvine to Inveraray	99 tons House Coal	Left June 1 Arr. June 1
Inveraray to Irvine	Ballast	Left June 3 Arr. June 3
Irvine to Inveraray	99 tons House Coal	Left June 8 Arr. June 9
Inverary to Irvine	Ballast	Left June 14 Arr. June 14
Irvine to Inveraray	100 tons House Coal	Left June 16 Arr. June 17
Inveraray to Irvine	Ballast	Left June 20 Arr. June 21
Irvine to Campbeltown	100 tons Bricks	Left June 24 Arr. June 24
Campbeltown to Irvine	Ballast	Left June 26 Arr. June 26
Irvine to Inveraray	100 tons House Coal	Left June 30 Arr. June 30

	Inveraray to Irvine	Ballast	Left June 8 Arr. June 8
	Irvine to Rothesay	85 tons House Coal	Left July 10 Arr. July 10
	Rothesay to Irvine	Ballast	Left July 15 Arr. July 16
	Irvine to Inveraray Inspected Inveraray 29/7/43	100 tons House Coal	Left July 26 Arr. July 27
	Inveraray to Irvine	Ballast	Left July 29 Arr. July 29
	Irvine to Inveraray	97 tons House Coal	Left July 30 Arr. July 31
	Inveraray to Ayr	Ballast	Left August 2 Arr. Aug. 3
	Ayr to Inveraray	94 tons House Coal	Left August 4 Arr. Aug. 5
	Inveraray to Ayr	Ballast	Left August 7 Arr. Aug. 9
	Ayr to Inveraray	100 tons House Coal	Left August 10 Arr. Aug. 11
	Inveraray to Irvine	Ballast	Left August 14 Arr. Aug. 14
	Irvine to Inveraray	98 tons House Coal	Left August 16 Arr. Aug. 17
	Inveraray to Irvine	Ballast	Left August 19 Arr. Aug. 21
	Irvine to Inveraray	97 tons House Coal	Left August 24 Arr. Aug. 24
	Inveraray to Carrickfergus Inspected C'fergus 27/8/43	Ballast	Left August 26 Arr. Aug. 27
	Carrickfergus to Belfast	Light	Left Spetember 29 Arr. Sep. 29
	Belfast to Irvine	74 tons Scrap Iron	Left October 6 Arr. Oct. 9
	Irvine to Inveraray	100 tons House Coal	Left October 13 Arr. Oct. 14
	Inveraray to Irvine	Ballast	Left October 15 Arr. Oct. 17
	Irvine to Campbeltown	99 tons Bricks	Left October 18 Arr. Oct. 23
	Campbeltown to Irvine	Ballast	Left November 1 Arr. Nov. 1
	Irvine to Inveraray	97 tons House Coal	Left November 3 Arr. Nov. 4
	Inveraray to Irvine	Ballast	Left November 6 Arr. Nov. 7
	Irvine to Inveraray	96 tons House Coal	Left November 13 Arr. Nov. 14
	Inverary to Irvine	Ballast	Left November 16 Arr. Nov. 17
	Irvine to Inveraray	95 tons House Coal	Left November 18 Arr. Nov. 20
	Inveraray to Irvine	Ballast	Left December 4 Arr. Dec. 5
	Irvine to Inveraray	100 tons House Coal	Left December 9 Arr. Dec. 10
	Inveraray to Irvine	Ballast	Left December 11 Arr. Dec. 12
	Irvine to Lamlash	100 tons Lime	Left December 14 Arr. Dec. 15
	Lamlash to Irvine	Ballast	Left December 16 Arr. Dec. 18
1944	Irvine to Brodick	100 tons Lime	Left January 18 am Arr. Jan. 18 pm
	Brodick to Irvine	Ballast	Left January 20 am Arr.Jan. 26 am

Irvine to Campbeltown	95 tons House Coal	Left February 2 am Arr. Feb. 2 pm
Campbeltown to Irvine	Ballast	Left February 10 am Arr. Feb. 10 pm
Irvine to Brodick	100 tons Limestone	Left February 11 am Arr. Feb.11 pm
Brodick to Irvine	Ballast	Left February 14 pm Arr. Feb.14 pm.
Irvine to Strachur	95 tons House Coal	Left February 16 am Arr. Feb.17 am
Strachur to Irvine	Ballast	Left Feb. 19 am Arr. Feb. 20 pm
Irvine to Rothesay	85 tons House Coal	Left February 21 am Arr. Feb. 21 pm
Rothesay to Irvine	Ballast	Left February 23 am Arr. Feb. 23 pm
Irvine to Ardrishaig	100 tons House Coal	Left February 23 am Arr. Feb. 24 am
Ardrishaig to Irvine	Ballast	Left February 26 am Arr. Feb. 26 pm
Irvine to Campbeltown	100 tons Bricks	Left March 3 am Arr. Mar. 3 pm
Campbeltown to Irvine	Ballast	Left March 6 am Arr. Mar 7 am
Irvine to Strachur	83 tons House Coal	Left March 9 am Arr. Mar. 9 pm
Strachur to Irvine	Ballast	Left March 11 pm Arr. Mar.12 am
Irvine to Millport	70 tons Limestone	Left March 25 am Arr. Mar. 25 pm
Millport to Irvine	Ballast	Left March 29 pm Arr. Mar. 29 pm
Irvine to Campbeltown	7 tons Bricks	Left March 30 am Arr. Mar. 30 pm
Campbeltown to Irvine	Ballast	Left April 3 am Arr. Apr. 3 pm
Irvine to Strachur	97 tons House Coal	Left April 4 pm Arr. Apr. 5 pm
Strachur to Irvine	Ballast	Left April 7 pm Arr. Apr. 8 am
Irvine to Campbeltown	95 tons General Cargo	Left April 12 am Arr. Apr. 12 pm
Campbeltown to Irvine	Ballast	Left April 15 am Arr. Apr. 15 pm
Irvine to Ardrishaig Inspected 26/4/44 Ardrishaig	99 tons House Coal	Left April 25 am Arr. Apr. 25 pm
Ardrishaig to Irvine	Ballast	Left Apr. 28 am Arr. Apr. 28 pm
Irvine to Campbeltown	93 tons Bricks	Left May 3 pm Arr. May 4 am
Campbeltown to Irvine	Ballast	Left May 10 am Arr. May 10 pm
Irvine to Rothesay	85 tons House Coal	Left June 20 am Arr. June 20 pm
Rothesay to Irvine	Ballast	Left June 24 am Arr. June 24 am

Irvine to Campbeltown	96 tons House Coal	Left July 1 am Arr. July 1 pm
Campbeltown to Irvine	Ballast	Left July 6 am Arr. July 6 pm
Irvine to Campbeltown	92 tons Bricks	Left July 7 pm Arr. July 7 pm
Campbeltown to Irvine	Ballast	Left July 11 am Arr. July 11 pm
Irvine to Campbeltown	100 tons Generals	Left July 12 Arr. July 12
Campbeltown to Irvine	Ballast	Left July 14 Arr. July 14
Irvine to Campbeltown	100 tons Generals	Left July 18 Arr. July 19
Campbeltown to Irvine	Ballast	Left July 22 Arr. July 22
Irvine to Strachur	89 tons Coal	Left July 24 Arr. July 24
Strachur to Irvine	Ballast	Left July 27 Arr. July 27
Irvine to Sharpness	Ballast	Left August 2 Arr. August 8

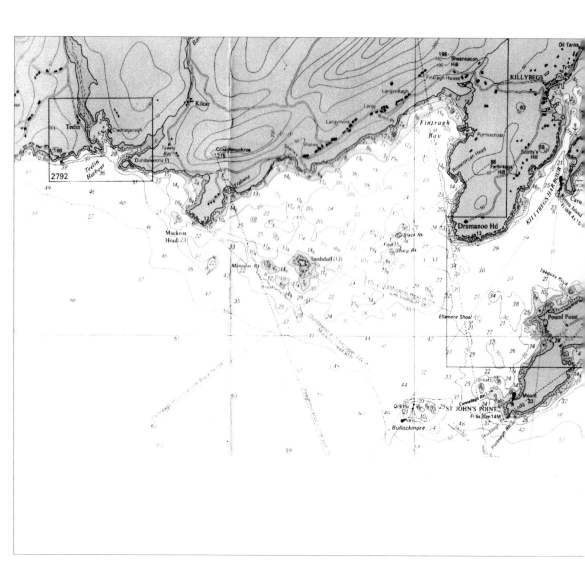

Appendix C

Admiralty Chart:
Courtesy Ewan McCullough
14 Clare Heights
Ballyclare
Co. Antrim

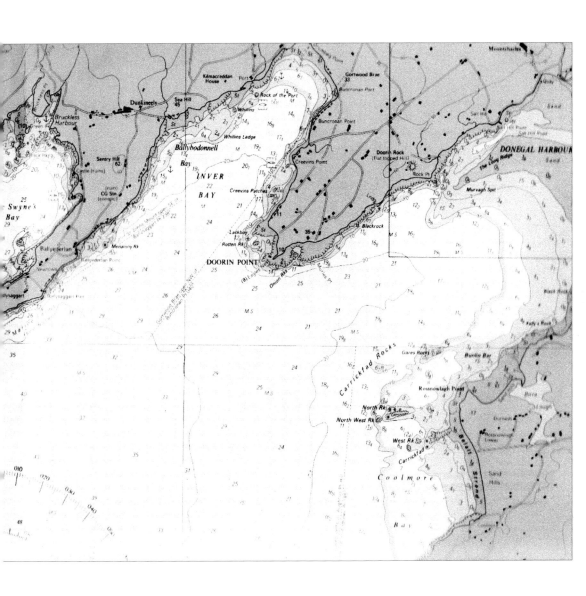

Appendix D

Map of Ireland based on Ordnance Survey Scale
Permision to copy granted by J. Sharkey OSNI. 23.2.2005

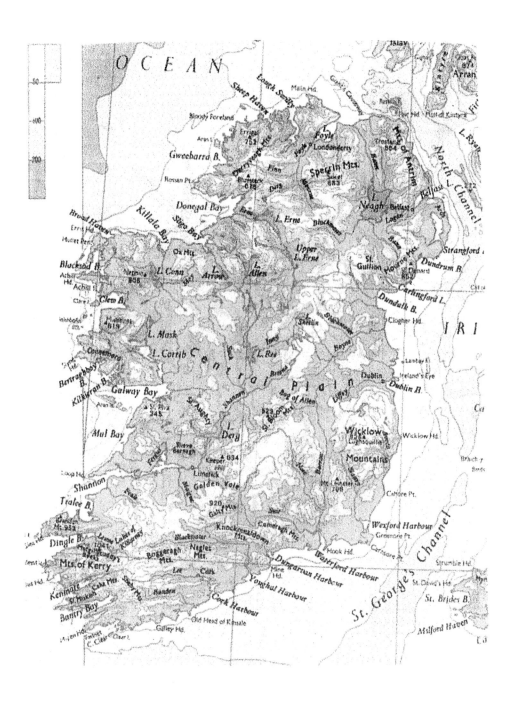

Ireland

1. Annalong
2. Kilkeel
3. Rostrevor
4. Warrenpoint
5. Omeath Beach
6. Giles Quay
7. Dundalk
8. Clogherhead
9. Drogheda
10. Balbriggan
11. Skerries
12. Dublin
13. Wicklow
14. Arklow
15. Courtown
16. Wexford
17. Waterford
18. New Ross
19. Ballycotton
20. Whitegate
21. Cork
22. Belmullet
23. Ballina
24. Ballinacurra
25. Sligo
26. Mullaghmore
27. Mullinasole
28. Donegal
29. Bruckless
30. Killybegs
31. Claddaghnageera
32. Teelin
33. Burtonport
34. Bunbeg
35. Downings
36. Mulroy Bay
37. Letterkenny
38. Buncrana
39. Deny
40. Coleraine
41. Carnlough
42. Carrickfergus
43. Belfast
44. Bangor
45. Portavogie
46. Portaferry
47. Kircubbin
48. Ringniel
49. Ballydoran
50. Ringhaddy
51. Strangford
52. Castleward
53. Quoile Quay

Great Britain

54. Plymouth
55. Truro
56. Bridgewater
57. Bristol
58. Sharpness
59. Gloucester
60. Newport
61. Cardiff
62. Barry Dock
63. Port Talbot
64. Neath
65. Swansea
66. Llanelli
67. Saundersfoot
68. Pembroke Dock
69. Milford Haven
70. Penrhyn
71. Connahs Quay
72. Ellesmere Port
73. Manchester
74. Liverpool
75. Garston
76. Preston
77. Whitehaven
78. Harrington
79. Workington
80. Maryport
81. Dalbeattie
82. Port William
83. Girvan
84. Ayr
85. Troon
86. Irvine
87. Ardrossan
88. Millport
    (Great Cumbrae Island)
89. Greenock
90. Glasgow
91. Bowling
92. Dumbarton
93. Rothesay. (Isle of Bute)
94. Kilchattin Bay
    (Isle of Bute)
95. Brodick (Isle of Arran)
96. Lamlash (Isle of Arran)
97. Whiting Bay
    (Isle of Arran)
98. Loch Striven
99. Strachur (Loch Fyne)
100. Inveraray (Loch Fyne)
101. Crarae (Loch Fyne)
102. Ardrishaig (Kintyre)
103. Tarbert (Kintyre)
104. Campbeltown (Kintre)

Isle of Man

105. Ramsey
106. Douglas
107. Castletown
108. Port St. Mary

Appendix E

Map of Ireland and West Coast of Britain based on Ordnance Survey Scale.

Permission to copy granted by J. Sharkey OSNI. 23.2.2005.

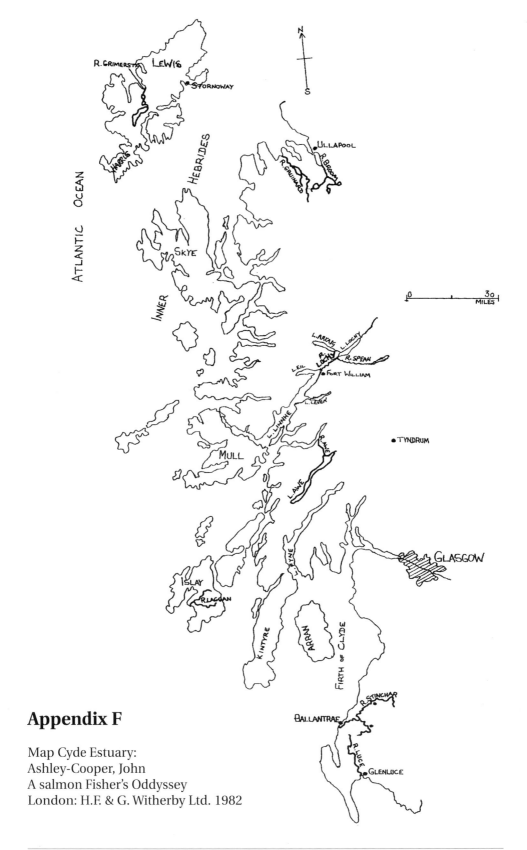

Appendix F

Map Cyde Estuary:
Ashley-Cooper, John
A salmon Fisher's Oddyssey
London: H.F. & G. Witherby Ltd. 1982

Appendix G

Map Severn Estuary:
Eglinton, Edmund
The Last of the Sailing Coasters
London: National Maritime Museum, HMSO 1982.

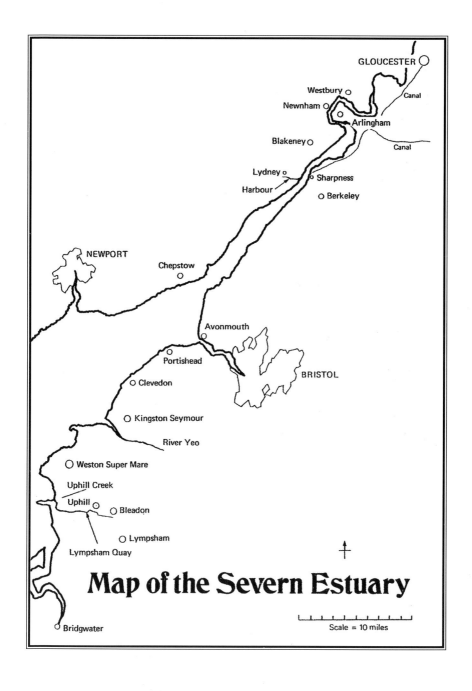

Map of the Severn Estuary

Scale = 10 miles

ACKNOWLEDGEMENTS

I am deeply indebted to the following for their help and support during my research of this work:

Walter Beyer, Bankhall Road, Magheramourne, Larne, Co. Antrim.

Diarmuid Bryce, Knocklyon Avenue, Templeogue, Dublin.

Brigid Cannon, Portachran, Kilcar, Co. Donegal.

Hugh Chesnutt, Derrylaghan, Kilcar, Co. Donegal.

Irene Coyle, Cloghan, Brockagh, Co. Donegal.

Catherine Cunningham, Kille, Kilcar, Co. Donegal.

Moira Cunningham, Claddaghnageera, Kilcar, Co. Donegal.

Kitty (Sean) Cunningham, Croaghlin, Teelin, Co. Donegal

Gerry Doyle, Moor Road, Kilkeel, Co. Down.

Joe Gallagher, An Sean Ceidh, Rann Na Cille, Teileann, Co. Dhún na nGall.

Judith Godfrey, Corry House, Kents Road, Torquay, Devon.

John Goût, Fron, Wellwood Drive, Dinas Powys, Vale of Glamorgan (Deceased)

Vernon Hegarty, Largymore, Kilcar, Co. Donegal.

Kenneth King, Straid Gallery, Glencolmcille, Co. Donegal.

John Lynch, Department of Modern History, Queen's University, Belfast.

Malachy Marken, Imagine Media Productions Ltd. 621 Lisburn Road, Belfast.

Elizabeth McBride, Harbour Road, Annalong, Co. Down.

Micheal Mac Giolla Easpuic, An Rualagh, Cill Cartha, Co. Dhún na nGall

Charley McCarthy, Point House, Point Road, Dundalk, Co. Louth.

Michael McCaughan, Ulster Folk and Transport Museum, Cultra, Co. Down.

Bernard McCaughey, Cedar Avenue, Belfast.

Ewan McCullough, Clare Heights, Ballyclare, Co. Antrim.

Mary McGeown, The Cottages, Kilcar, Co. Donegal.

Sam McKibbin, River Road, Lambeg, Co. Antrim.

Uel McKibbin, Chimera Wood, Helen's Bay. Co. Down.

Anthony McNelis, Ballymore, Teelin, Co. Donegal.

Michael McShane, Cloghan, Brockagh, Co. Donegal.

James Parsons, Victoria Street, Armagh.

Lulu Chesnutt
October 2006.